MOMENTS IN TIME

50 Years of Associated Press News Photos

ANGUS & ROBERTSON PUBLISHERS

ANGUS & ROBERTSON PUBLISHERS

Unit 4, Eden Park, 31 Waterloo Road,
North Ryde, NSW, Australia 2113
and
16 Golden Square, London W1R 4BN, United Kingdom

First published in the United States of America as *Moments In Time*
by The Associated Press, in 1984.

This revised edition first published in Australia by Angus & Robertson
Publishers and in the United Kingdom by Angus & Robertson (UK) Ltd in 1984.

Copyright © The Associated Press, New York, 1984

ISBN 0 207 14980 1

Project Director: Dan Perkes
Photo Editor: Hal Buell
Editor/Writer: Norm Goldstein
Photo Researcher: Wendy L. Davis
Darkroom Technician: Benjamin Schiff
Design: Harry Chester Associates
Typography: TypeCast Inc.
Photos by the staff and member newspaper
photographers of The Associated Press

Printed in Hong Kong

Foreword

"The keen historic spasm of the shutter." —James Agee.

A good picture is an art form and a good news picture can tell an entire story. Little if anything else can evoke the past so powerfully and so completely as a photograph.

This book is dedicated to the professional photographers of The Associated Press and its member newspapers, and the free-lancers and amateurs who have dedicated themselves to that end; to those who died in the pursuit; to those who tracked history with courage and talent and thus extended human vision.

Keith Fuller
President and General Manager
The Associated Press

Moments . . .

Moments in time . . .

. . . a great airship bursts into flames and turns to rubble on a New Jersey field . . . a human reaches out to touch another human on a window ledge high above a city street . . . a soldier raises his pistol and executes an enemy . . . horses, black images on a background of brilliant, new snow . . . fluttering, ample white skirts on a movie set in New York. . . .

Each is a moment in time, a microsecond isolated forever by a news photographer.

The still picture is just that, a moment in time . . . memorable, lasting, a fraction of a second isolated from the many other seconds. It is there forever to consider, ponder, re-examine.

Still pictures are recalled by most of us because they retain images the way our mind captures them—as single frames of memory of a person or an event.

Unlike the fleeting glimpse that television provides, the still picture provides each of us the opportunity to dwell on the meaning, the message, perhaps the beauty of the single moment.

Thus, a book of photographs, to set down permanently a picture record of some of the great events and moments of the last half-century. It seemed fitting to do this as The Associated Press marked the 50th anniversary of its still picture network.

What to include in this collection?

We started by saying that only pictures with intrinsic photographic worth would be included. But news events and the sheer force of history frequently interceded. We ended up with a mix of pictures of high photographic value, and pictures of great significance.

To our delight there were many instances in which both criteria were satisfied.

Consider the AP picture from Vietnam by Eddie Adams of a Viet Cong being executed by a Vietnamese general. It, along with several others printed in this book, are symbolic of the Vietnam war. It was a moment of great importance, and it was also recorded by a television camera; a film sequence that few recall.

Consider Marilyn Monroe on that subway grating as she prepared for a scene in "The Seven Year Itch" . . . the gentle updraft and another moment in time. Today's women of the screen, silver and phosphorous, show much more. But that flutter of white skirt will set off a series of remembrances difficult to match by either today's string bikini or a newsrack full of skin mags.

Not all the pictures in this book, we concluded, should be momentous because not all of the some two million photos a publication would have received since 1935 were momentous. Not all were of historical events, or of life-and-death situations, caught in the freeze of a microsecond.

Thus, we included moments of quiet beauty, and moments wherein the incident or the juxtaposition of people and things struck us as humorous or insightful.

In some cases several photographs emerged from a single event—each a special moment in itself. In other instances, several photographs made years apart served to demonstrate that the past is, indeed, prologue, and that news is the daily thread of history.

Thus Queen Elizabeth is coronated and waves from a balcony, her young, first born son at her side. Decades later the same group stands on a balcony of the same building in London. But the child-to-be-king now stands with his bride, Lady Diana.

Thus from Moscow, a series of pictures, each showing a Communist leader's coffin carried on the shoulders of those who would follow him . . . in the hierarchy and in the bier. A grim reminder of man's mortality and time's inevitable progress.

Great photography? Intrinsically of fine photographic merit? Probably not. But truly memorable moments in time along the thread of history.

So the selection process became more difficult as the considerations stacked one upon the other, then intertwined, then jumped decades, then touched on history, then news, then photographic worth.

In the end, no doubt, the final selections contained some subjective input.

Many of the photos in this book were made by staff photographers of The Associated Press. But the nature of news pictures and the need for speed in transporting them from here to there demands a resource that transcends any staff, no matter the size.

Thus, many of the pictures originate with other than AP staff . . . from the photographers of AP member newspapers who provide the AP with most of its pictures . . . from stringers and from freelancers who happened to see a special moment, either by accident or design . . . from the photographers of other picture agencies with which The AP works . . . sometimes from amateurs who were caught up in a great event, or a telling incident.

There is no limit to the sources for The AP wires and there was no limit to the sources we sought out for picture considerations; only that the picture had appeared on the AP photo wire during the period since 1935.

FIRST WIREPHOTO was an airview of a plane crash in the Adirondack Mountains in New York state. It was sent on the AP Wirephoto network when 1935 was just hours old.

What of AP Wirephoto, or AP Laserphoto as it is now called?

There is little debate anywhere that the concept revolutionized daily picture journalism. And for one single reason: After 1935, news photographs from many places in the United States, and later from the world, showed today's events in today's newspapers.

Before 1935 and Wirephoto's inception, days, sometimes weeks, would pass before pictures of significant events reached the desks of daily newspapers.

AP Wirephoto changed that forever. It delivered photos quickly and did for daily journalism what aircraft did for the traveler.

It is a kind of technological miracle that pictures are transmitted at all. Each photo must be broken into some 2¼ million microscopic mosaics, each mosaic converted into electronic energy, then sent across a wire, then reassembled again in precise order on photographic material at the receiving end . . . or at the many receiving ends.

This electronic journey, which takes some 10 minutes, may begin in a fine, sophisticated photo lab in Stockholm, or Washington, Kalamazoo, or Kuala Lumpur . . . or it may begin in a steamy jungle town, aboard a ship at sea, in a stadium toilet converted to a temporary photo lab, or in a motel room in a forgotten town on a forgotten highway.

It started 50 years ago, early on New Year's Day, 1935. Considerable effort was expended to stitch together a telephone line that linked 47 newspapers in

JOE ROSENTHAL, AP photographer who took the famous Iwo Jima flag-raising picture, went back to look over the scene. The Marine Corps took his picture.

WIREPHOTO EQUIPMENT used at the start of the network in 1935 is shown here. The picture to be transmitted is mounted on the cylinder of the sending machine in the rear.

25 American cities on a wire that would be open daily for the exclusive transmission of photos.

Pictures had been transmitted before that. In fact, American Telephone and Telegraph had attempted to set up a picture network for public use, but it failed for lack of business. In some foreign countries today such public networks exist, and The AP uses them to connect picture transmissions to AP's vast network.

But back to 1935. . . . The first photo to be transmitted on this network was an airview of a plane crash in upstate New York. The transmission was completed flawlessly. A newspaper that has been on that network since then has received over two million photographs virtually non-stop during the passage of half a century.

The network has changed, of course, in 50 years. Thousands of picture receivers are linked to subnetworks in the United States, Europe, Africa, and the Middle East, South America, Asia, Australia.

These subnetworks are connected by satellite circuits or undersea cables which make the AP picture network fully and instantly international.

Pictures flash across these circuits 24 hours a day with sophisticated editorial decisions sending them to only one American state or a single European nation, or to the whole world. A picture can be transmitted from Bangkok and drop out of thousands of receivers simultaneously around the globe.

But all the electronic wizardry and the tens of thousands of miles of circuitry are mere tools in the hands of the editors and photographers who stand the watch on world events.

Those who would put down news photography say that great pictures like these are a matter of luck.

And photographers themselves, frequently say that instinct plays a great part in the making of pictures that capture memorable moments in time.

Perhaps. But it is also true that the harder photo people work the luckier they get. And Louis Pasteur, when told he was lucky to have discovered pasteurization, acknowledged that chance was a factor. But he added that chance favors the prepared mind.

Some have said that Joe Rosenthal was lucky when

HORST FAAS, AP photographer best known for his combat photos, won two Pulitzer Prizes, one for war pictures taken in Vietnam, the other in Bangladesh (with Michel Laurent).

he photographed the flag raising on Iwo Jima. Yes, good fortune played a role. But Rosenthal took the time to pile rocks atop one another to get a better angle; the light was diffused so that picture was fully lit in the shadows; the pipe to which the flag was attached was heavy and the men strained to put it up; the terrain was rough and torn as in war; the wind caught the banner just right. And as in Adams' Vietnam photo, this scene was filmed. But for anyone who was ever touched in any way by World War II, Rosenthal's moment in time is the only moment remembered.

As a group these photographers are not effete people. The rigors of photography do not generate men and women comfortable in the salon or at the diplomatic cocktail party, though their beat takes them to those places, too.

Most of us have seen the photographic push as a group of cameramen who struggle seemingly to shoot from exactly the same spot. Each attempts to instantly put together the proper composition, lighting, juxtaposition of people or things with a subject that will be gone in an instant, never to return.

More photographers died in Vietnam than any other media group. To find the pictures they had to go to the field. They found the pictures all right, but too many failed to return.

It is not a trade for the faint of heart.

Technology has assisted photographers greatly in the last decade and the mechanics of making pictures is comparatively simple. But much of picture taking is the same. There is still the cold and the heat; the too dry and the too wet; there remains the courage to face physical danger or the wrath of a pushed aside politician who stands between a photographer and real history; there remains the need to stay ever alert for

MODERN AP PICTURE transmitter; a room of equipment has been reduced to the size of a portable typewriter.

the turn or the twist or the special expression, for the precise combination of people and events.

The electronics . . . the technology . . . the circuits: these are mere tools. What counts—what will always count—are the editors and the photographers, and the moments in time.

—Hal Buell
—Assistant General Manager for Newsphotos
—The Associated Press

ELECTRONIC DARKROOM: Computerized pictures, shown on a TV screen, are handled by an editor today in seconds and sped to destinations around the world.

"...Sudden, Stark Tragedy"

It was May 6, 1937. A faint drizzle drifted down on the naval air station at Lakehurst, N.J., just off the Atlantic coast. It was about 7 p.m. when Capt. Max Pruss of the Hindenburg received word that he could land.

The Hindenburg, "the silvery queen of the skies," was about to complete its first trans-Atlantic flight of the season. The German-made zeppelin, inflated with hydrogen, had made 37 crossings to North and South America since going into service in 1936. Named after former German general and president Paul von Hindenburg, it had come to symbolize a resurgent Nazi Germany under Adolf Hitler.

It had left Frankfurt, Germany, three days earlier, but had been delayed by headwinds and, later, thunderstorms over New Jersey.

It carried 31 passengers and a crew of 69. For a $400 fare, the passengers got a luxurious trip aloft, complete with gourmet continental meals, a lounge, a bar, and 70 staterooms.

At 7:20 p.m., as the ground crew awaited below, the Hindenburg was 200 feet up, its nose approaching the mooring mast. The landing lines had been dropped to the rain-soaked ground.

Ten minutes later . . . a dull explosion near the tail . . . a bright flash of light.

Associated Press photographer Murray Becker was there, with other cameramen, to record the landing. He recalled:

"As I stood waiting for the zeppelin to swing around, a tongue of flame suddenly burst from the tail section. In the next second, the tail section exploded.

"I was stunned, but I caught the ship on an even keel before it crashed to the ground seconds later. I was conscious of a terrific blast of heat and of people screaming about me, but I ran forward, snapping pictures until the heat drove me back.

". . . Never had I seen such sudden, stark tragedy."

In 47 seconds, fire completely devoured the airship, reducing it to a flaming skeleton.

Thirteen passengers died. So did 22 of the crew and one of the ground crew.

Some, somehow, lived.

Investigations followed, with the probable cause said to be static electricity touching off some leaking hydrogen gas.

The real cause, however, was never determined.

Asian Agony

It was Aug. 28, 1937. H.S. Wong was the only cameraman left on the roof of an office building in Shanghai, where newsmen had awaited an expected Japanese attack on the blockaded Whampoo River. The Japanese had made almost daily bombing raids on Shanghai in their war against Chiang Kai-shek's troops.

Wong saw the bombs and then the black smoke coming from the South Railway station and rushed toward it.

By the time he got there, he saw only the dead, the dying, the maimed.

And this bloodied, crying child.

Dust Bowl

"Now the wind grew stronger and hard . . .

"Little by little the sky was darkened by the mixing dust, and the wind fell over the earth, loosened the dust and carried it away. The wind grew stronger. . . . .

"The finest dust did not settle back to earth now, but disappeared into the darkening sky."

John Steinbeck described the destructive dust storm in his book, "The Grapes of Wrath."

The dry winds had come in terrible reality in the 1930s and blew the dried-out topsoil into the air. It had hit Oklahoma and parts of Texas, creating a "dust bowl" and forcing thousands of farmers to leave their homes to seek sustenance elsewhere.

This famous photograph by Arthur Rothstein, taken in 1936, shows an Oklahoma farmer and his sons seeking shelter from the storm.

Hitler and Holocaust

By 1935, Adolf Hitler had sold his maniacal theories of a "superior race" to unhappy Germans and controlled the mass hysteria. His power was absolute, dictatorial and demonic.

Through fear and fanatic fervor, he was able to attract and sway huge crowds wherever he appeared. Here, then-Chancellor Hitler was cheered at Templehof Airport in Berlin as he arrived for a patriotic speech on Germany's National Labor Day, May 1, 1935.

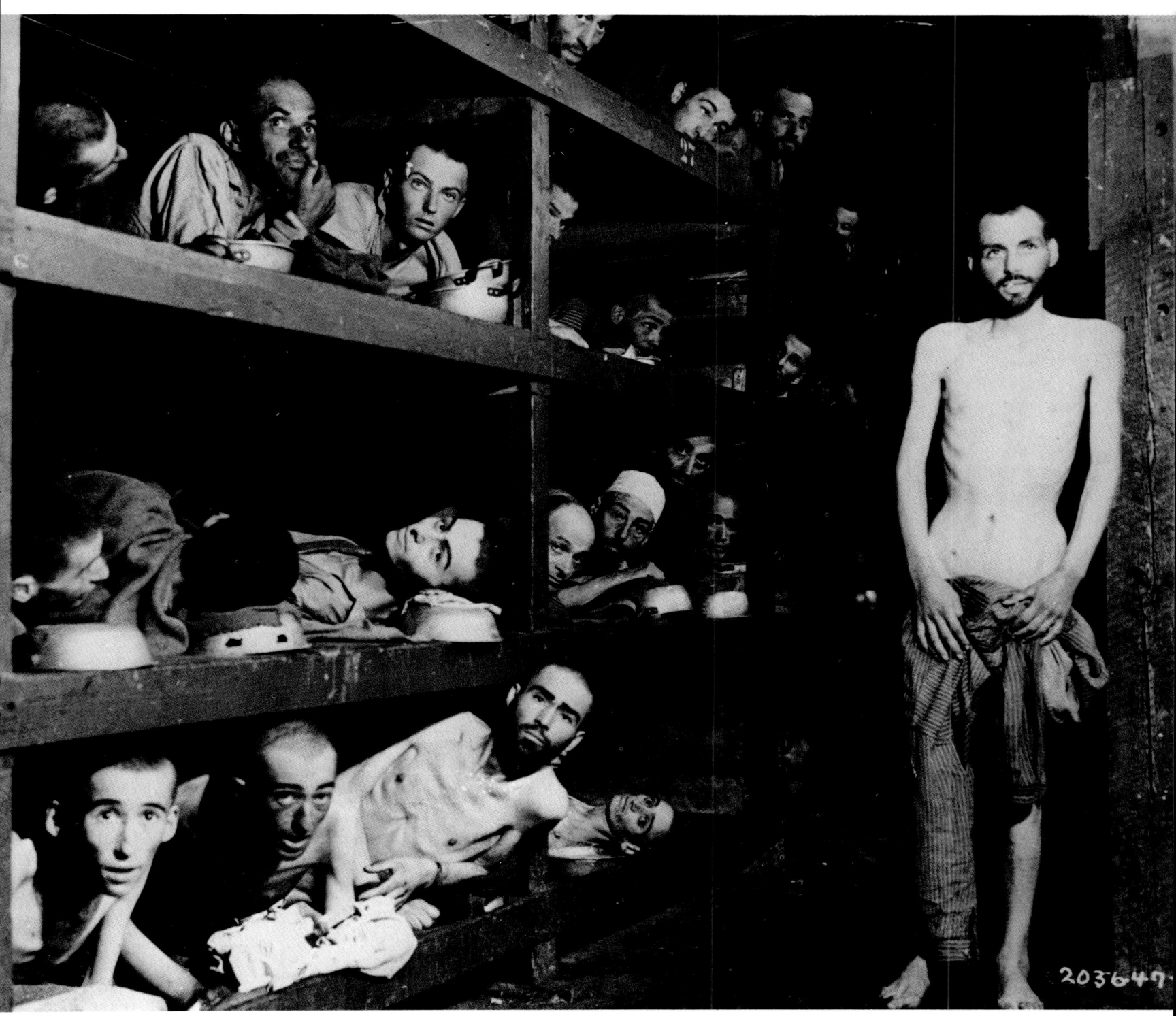

Ten years later, millions were dead, victims of his madness and methods.

When the second global war finally destroyed him and Germany surrendered to Allied troops, the horror of his dictatorship became ghastly evident.

These were slave laborers in the Buchenwald concentration camp. Millions had died in gas chambers and from malnutrition before U.S. troops of the 80th Division entered the camp to free them in April 1945.

World Champion

Few of the great athletic champions of this century have had such a powerful, significant and continuing hold on history as Jesse Owens.

The track star astonished Hitler's Germany and the world at the Berlin Olympics in 1936 by winning four gold medals: the long jump, 100-meter dash, 200-meter dash and as a member of the 400-meter relay team. The American athlete became known as the fastest man on earth—and a symbol of freedom in the face of Nazi Germany.

Behind him is German long-jumper Lutz Long, who placed second. It was Long who had raised Owens' arm to salute his triumph, to the chagrin of Hitler and other Nazis looking on. Owens and Long became lifelong friends.

Photo is by AP's Anthony Camerano.

Heavyweight of Champions

Formal acknowledgement of the superiority of a champion comes with a title, a crown of recognition. A few, a special few, become the stuff of legend, even folk heroes.

Joseph Louis Barrow—Joe Louis—was such a heavyweight among champions.

The man nicknamed the "Brown Bomber" took over the heavyweight boxing title of the world when he knocked out Jim Braddock in the 8th round on June 22, 1937. Louis defended the title a record 25 times before he retired nearly 12 years later, March 1, 1949. Perhaps his most memorable fight was the classic one-round destruction of Germany's Max Schmeling in 1938.

Here, he displays his power with a smashing left that lifts Tami Mauriello off both his feet in a title fight at Yankee Stadium on Sept. 13, 1946. Louis went on to knock out Mauriello in 2:09 of the first round as 29,000 fans watched.

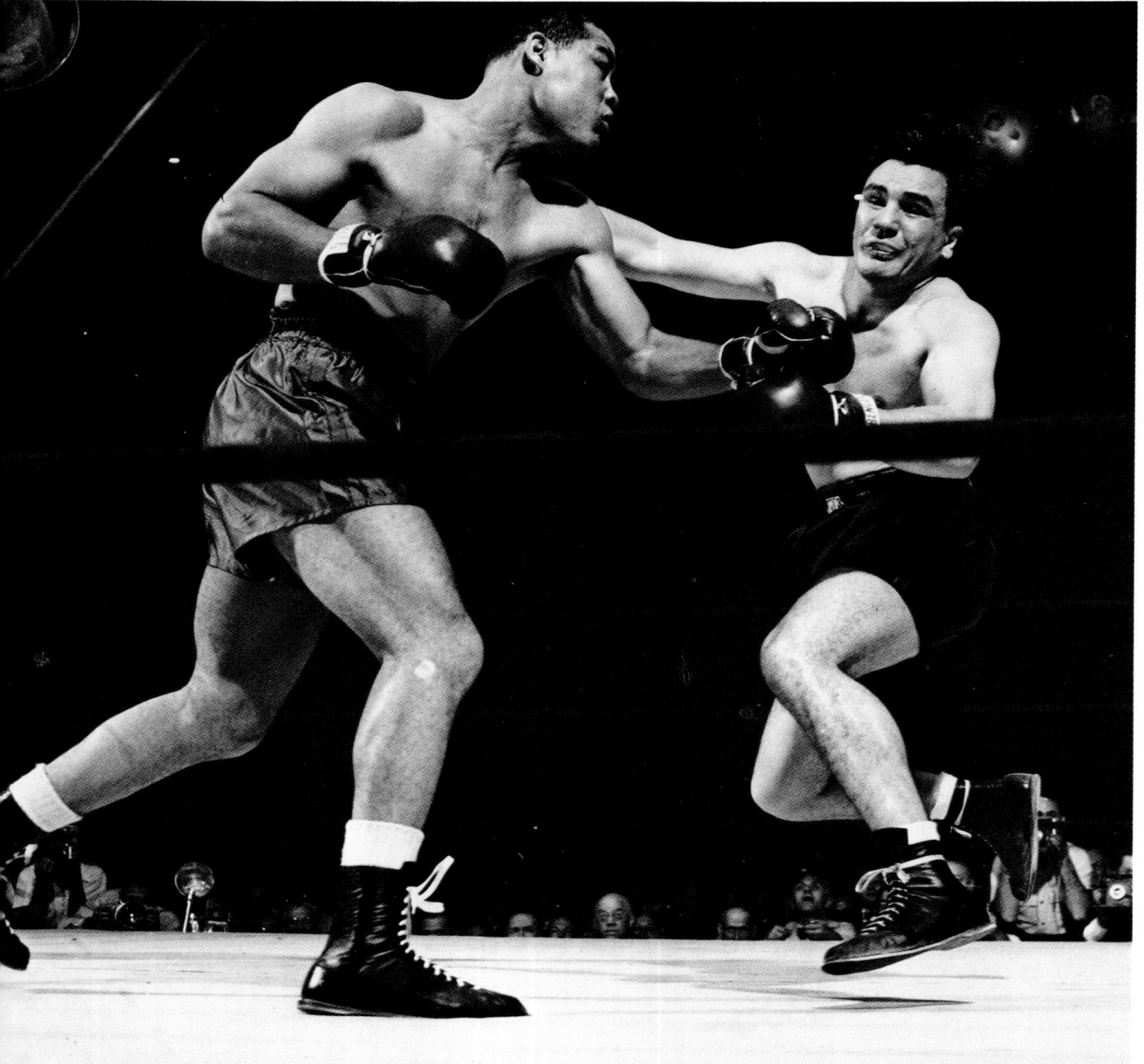

Baseball's Best Bow Out

On July 4, 1939, some 60,000 people packed Yankee Stadium to cheer, to remember, to cry, as they said goodbye to Lou Gehrig, the "Iron Man" who set the record of 2,130 consecutive games playing first base for the New York Yankees between June 1, 1925, and April 30, 1939, his last game.

His record-breaking career was cut short by amyotrophic lateral sclerosis, a debilitating and eventually fatal muscle illness. It came to be known as "Lou Gehrig's disease."

AP Photographer Murray Becker was there, too, to capture the moment. When it came time to say goodbye to his beloved game, tears came to Gehrig's eyes as he said: "I have been given a bad break, but I have an awful lot to live for."

He died in June 1941.

Babe Ruth was the very personification of baseball. Yankee Stadium is still known as "The House That Ruth Built."

The slugger's records may have since fallen, but somehow his 60 home runs in one year, his 714 in a career running from 1914 to 1948, somehow they seem still to be the hitter's heavens.

When fans and players came for the 25th anniversary celebration of Yankee Stadium on June 13, 1948, they gave the most vociferous ovation to the Sultan of Swat. In a raspy voice, the ailing Ruth said goodbye to the misty-eyed gathering.

They retired his No. 3 that day, but the memories of his milestones remain, memories revived by Harry Harris' photo of the farewell.

Ruth died of cancer two months later.

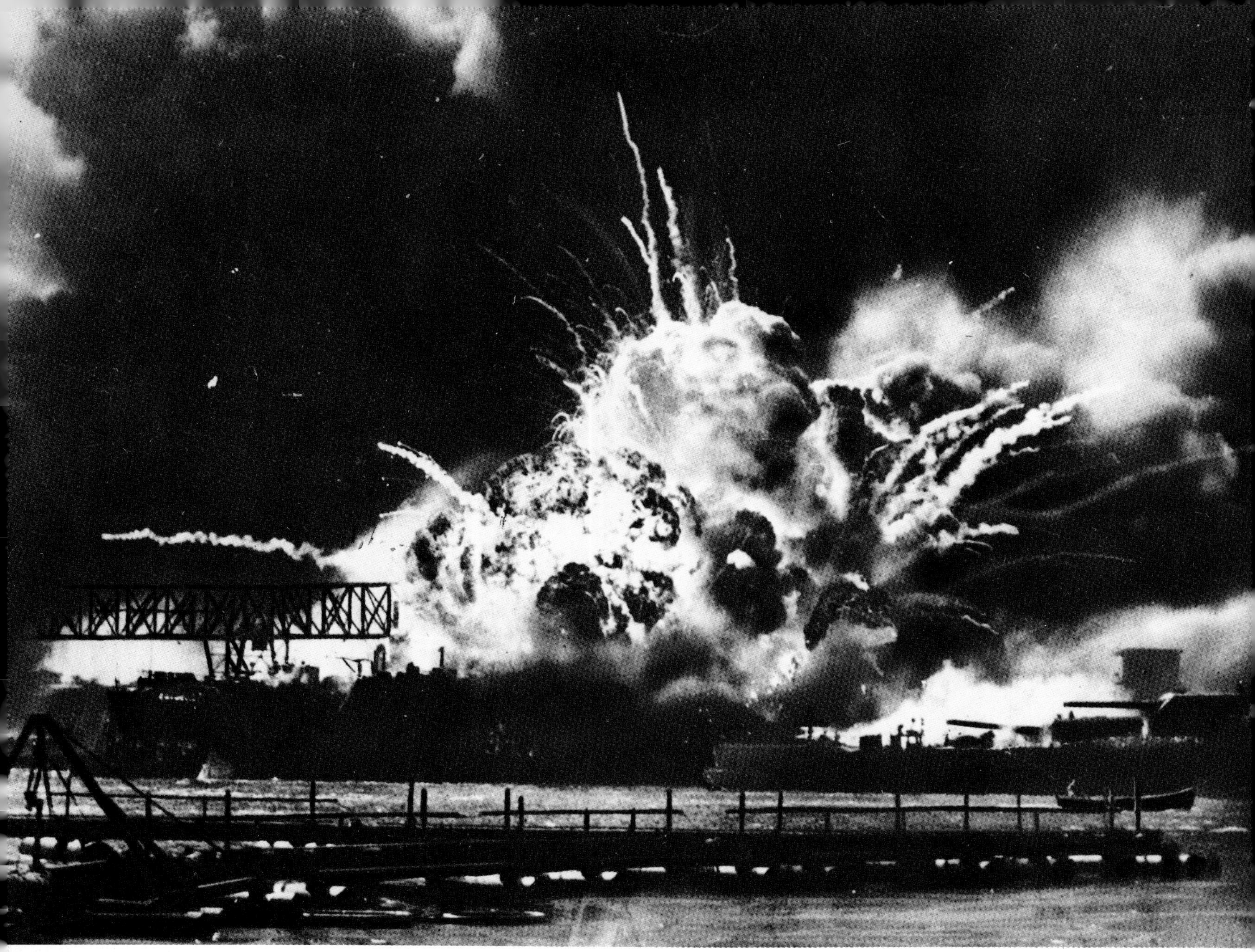

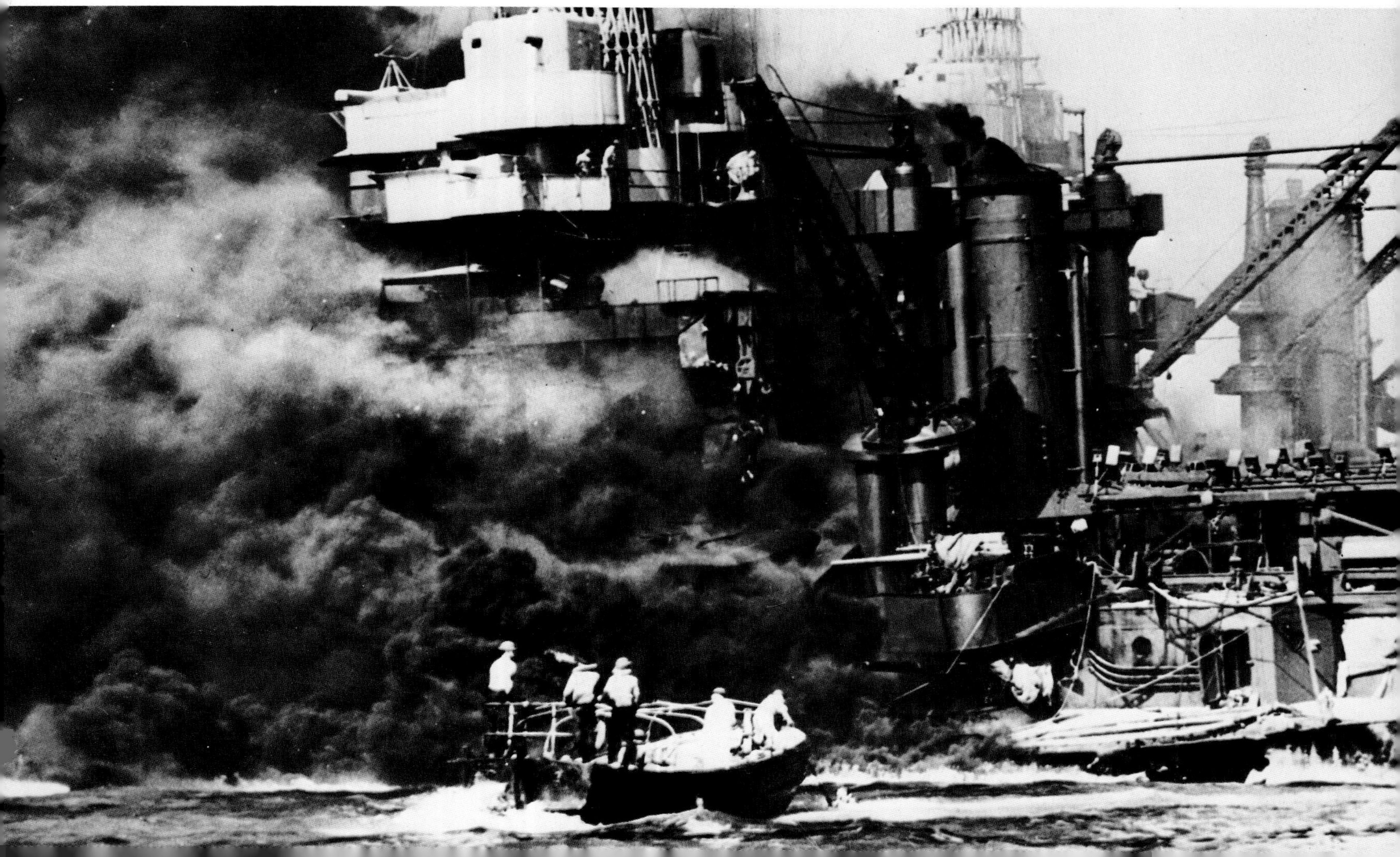

Pearl Harbor

At 7:53 a.m., Dec. 7, 1941, an air fleet of Japanese fighters, dive bombers and torpedo planes attacked U.S. airfields and the U.S. Pacific fleet at Pearl Harbor on the Hawaiian island of Oahu.

Another group of planes came half an hour later and continued the devastating surprise attack.

One thousand people were killed when a bomb struck and sunk the U.S.S. Arizona. The U.S.S. Oklahoma capsized. Fire spread through the battleship West Virginia, the carrier Enterprise, the battleship California.

In less than two hours, the main force of the U.S. Pacific fleet had been crippled. More than 2,400 U.S. servicemen were killed, another 1,000 wounded.

The next day, as President Roosevelt branded Dec. 7 as "a date which will live in infamy," the United States formally declared war on Japan. So did Great Britain. Three days later, Germany and Italy joined Japan and proclaimed war on the United States.

It was the beginning of nearly four years of global war.

Water, Water Everywhere...

AP photographer Frank "Pappy" Noel had filmed the British forces through their jungle retreat from the Japanese in Singapore. He was suffering from malaria. It was January 1942 and Singapore was about to fall.

Noel got on a British ship, but it was hit by a submarine torpedo at night, 270 miles out of port. For five days, he and 27 other survivors drifted in lifeboats under a withering sun.

He captured their plight in this Pulitzer Prize-winning photograph, taken when another lifeboat passed near his and an Indian sailor reached out, pleading for water.

Ultimately, they reached Sumatra.

One for Old Glory

Iwo Jima was one of a chain of islands in the South Pacific that meant a rough road to victory and the end of World War II.

The 60,000 Marines who stormed the island on Feb. 19, 1945, met savage opposition from the ensconced Japanese. Then, on Feb. 23, they took the high ground. At 10:15 that morning, they raised a small United States flag at the top of Mount Suribachi, 550 feet above the sea.

Associated Press photographer Joe Rosenthal was there, too, right at the peak of the action.

For the 28th Regiment, Fifth Division Marines, the symbolic flag was not big enough. A patrol took up another one, 5-by-8 feet, twice as large as the first.

"As I got closer," Rosenthal was to recall, "I saw a group of our men hauling a long iron pipe, and then I discovered still another Marine holding a neatly folded American flag."

Rosenthal, only 5-feet-5, backed away and stacked some stones on a sandbag from a Japanese bunker so he could see over the lip of the crater where he stood.

He leveled his bulky Speed Graphic and, as the Marines lunged forward, driving the new flag into the ground, Rosenthal caught the moment that transcended its time and place and became an instant frozen in history.

Eventually, a huge sculpture of that photograph would be cast in bronze as a symbol of victory and valor.

Rosenthal's famous photo won the Pulitzer Prize in 1945.

A Mac Attack

After a forced departure from the Philippines, Gen. Douglas MacArthur dramatically announced, "I shall return."

And return he did.

In September 1943, a U.S. Signal Corps photographer caught the general in typically theatrical action as he looked out the gun port of a Flying Fortress over New Guinea.

There, paratroopers dropped into the Markham Valley jungle to begin Operation Cartwheel, an island-hopping military venture that was the first step toward realizing MacArthur's promise.

The Champs

Paris is free again. On Aug. 29, 1944, four days after the liberation of the French capital, some 15,000 American soldiers marched down the Champs Elysee, the Arc de Triomphe in the background, in a show of force. Associated Press photographer Peter J. Carroll on this day shared the back of an Army truck with another AP photographer, Harry Harris. They tossed a coin for the shot. Carroll made the picture.

Il Pleut,
Le Monde Pleut

It was the worst of times in Western Europe.
Nazi forces had taken Norway, the Netherlands, Belgium and France. England was rocked by daily bombings.

It was February 1941. In Marseilles, spectators watched with unrestrained emotions as the flags of defeated French regiments were carried to the docks, on the way to Algeria for safe keeping.

"Big Three" at Yalta

British Prime Minister Winston Churchill, U.S. President Franklin D. Roosevelt and Soviet Premier Josef Stalin gathered at the Livadia Palace at Yalta in Russia's Crimea in February 1945 to discuss the end of World War II. The Big Three powers reached agreements at that conference that changed the course of world events.

East Meets West

The Elbe River begins in Czechoslovakia and flows north through central Germany to the North Sea. In 1945, it became the symbol of a significant moment in history.

American troops, crossing the Rhine into the heart of Germany in March 1945, reached the Elbe in April. There, they met Russian soldiers who had come from the east.

Helmeted infantrymen of the U.S. First Army greeted their Soviet counterparts on a broken bridge over the Elbe at Torgau, Germany. It meant the German Reich was cut in two; it was the symbolic end of World War II in Europe.

On May 7—V-E Day for Victory in Europe—the Germans officially surrendered.

Tarawa Island

Midway. Guadalcanal. Coral and Bismarck Seas. The island-hopping battles of the Pacific, in all their deadly cost, continued inexorably late into 1943.

In November, it was another of the Gilbert Island chain: Tarawa

AP photographer Frank Filan recorded the results of the combat in this Pulitzer Prize winner, which seems permeated with the stench of the Japanese bodies strewn about a blasted pillbox after the U.S. Marine invasion.

Victory

It was a week after two atomic bombs were dropped on Japan. The war was indeed finally over.

Let the celebration begin.

In New York, civilians and service personnel jammed just about every inch of Times Square on Aug. 14, 1945, waved American flags and shouted their joy after they heard the official announcement that Japan had surrendered.

Bikini Bomb Blast

The Bikini atoll, a ring of 27 small islands around a lagoon in the Pacific, was the site of atom bomb tests made by the United States in July 1946.

The native population of the two-square mile island halfway between Hawaii and New Guinea was removed to another island, but 70 ships were left in the lagoon for testing and experiments.

The photo, from Joint Task Force One, shows the explosion of the atomic bomb dropped from the superfortress Dave's Dream on July 1. The picture was made from a tower on Bikini Island by a remote control camera recording automatic pictures of the blast, part of "Operation Crossroads."

29

Avery Hauled

"We told Mr. Avery he would have to leave. Mr. Avery refused."

The speaker was Francis Biddle, the U.S. attorney general on that April 27, 1944.

The "Mr. Avery" was Sewell Avery, chairman of Montgomery Ward & Co.

The stalemate was over a government effort to get Avery to extend an expired labor contract to end a strike and get workers back to helping the war effort.

Finally, the U.S. government brought in the Army.

Associated Press photographer Harry Hall was outside Chicago headquarters of Montgomery Ward when Sgt. Jacob Lepak and Pvt. Cecil Dies hauled Avery out.

Zut! Zoot Suit!

"Reet pleat . . . drape shape . . . zoot suit."

The lyrics from a popular song of the early 1940s (remember Cab Calloway?) described the flashy fashion of the time, one later picked up and identified with young male gangs in the larger cities.

The suits, typically, were thigh-length jackets with wide padded shoulders and narrow cuffs on the trousers. The style apparently came from black jazz musicians and was trendy among youthful Damon Runyon types during World War II.

In this photo, zoot gangsters were portrayed by actors in a movie being made at Universal Studios. The War Production Board had banned the sale of zoot suits because they required the use of more material than the average suit, but an exception was made for the film.

Wrong Nose

Referee Lee Sala got a little too close to the action during a bout between Willie Chaney and John Pinney in Tampa, Fla., in 1973.

Sala got a shot in the nose, but was not injured, when Chaney's punch went past Pinney. Pinney won by a TKO. The ref was around to make the decision.

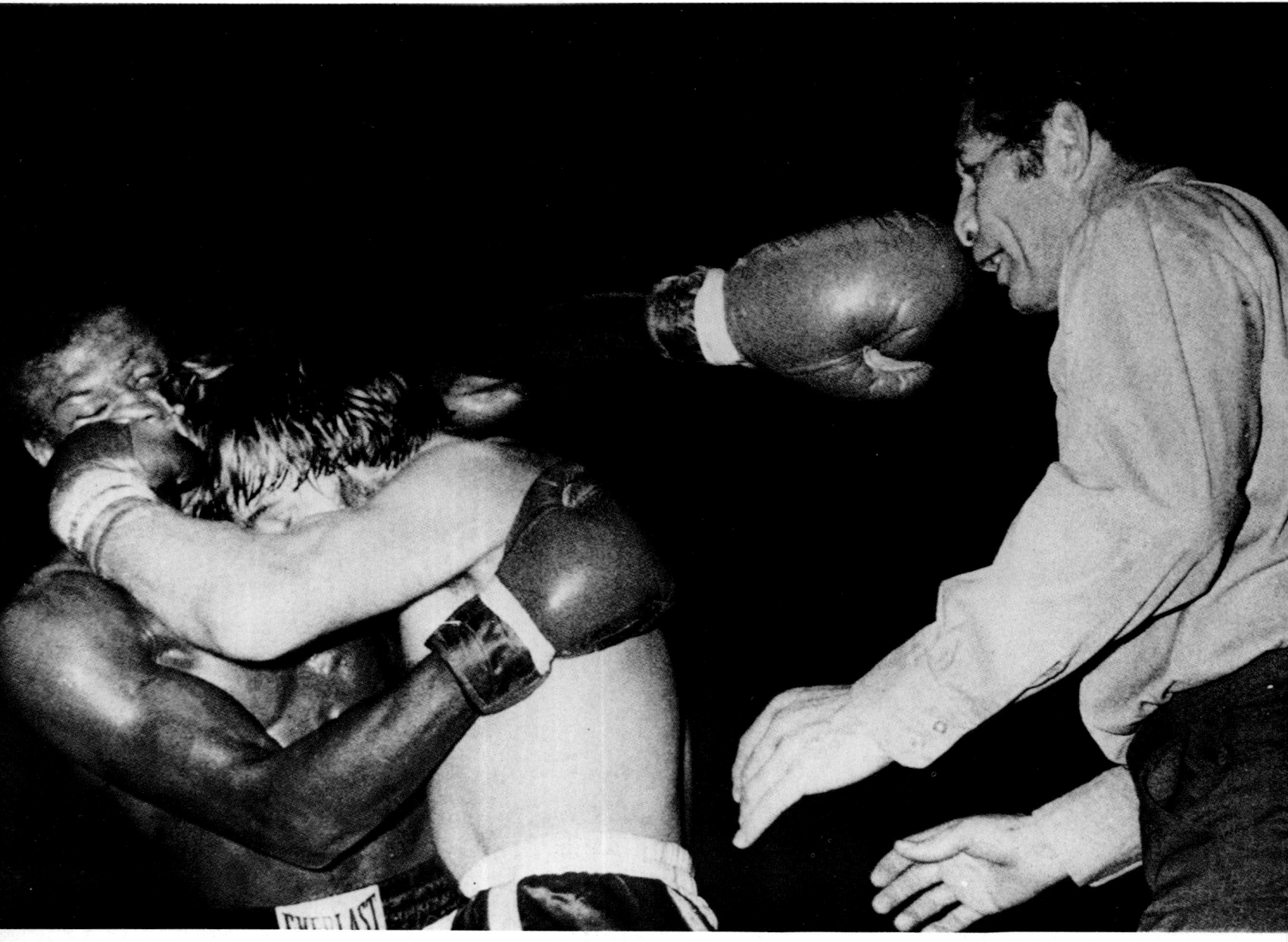

Watchdogs

Two pug mugs meet as J. Edgar Hoover, FBI director, greets Holly Spring, boxer entered in a dog show in Washington, in April 1954.
(Photo by Bill Smith.)

Check That, Please

Harry S. Truman is laughing at what appears to be a banner announcement of his defeat. The chuckle is because he knew better.

The final returns in the November 1948 presidential election showed Truman with 24,179,345 votes to Gov. Thomas Dewey's 21,991,291. The voters has buried predictions of writers, pollsters and politicians, all of whom had expected Dewey to win.

Returning to Washington from his home in Independence, Mo., aboard his "Victory Special" train, Truman stopped in St. Louis where he was handed the early edition of the Chicago Tribune.

(Photo by AP's Byron Rollins.)

Missouri Waltz?

The tinkler of the keys is none other than President Harry Truman, who would often entertain on the White House piano.

The lady of the legs is actress Lauren Bacall, who is not teaching the president how to whistle.

The occasion was Miss Bacall's appearance at the National Press Club canteen in Washington, D.C., early in 1945.

Teacher and Disciple

A bespectacled Mohandas Gandhi, the Mahatma, who eventually led India to its independence, enjoyed a laugh with the man who was to be the nation's first prime minister, Jawaharlal Nehru. The occasion was the All-India Congress committee meeting in Bombay, India, July 6, 1946. Nehru took office as president of the Congress during the session.

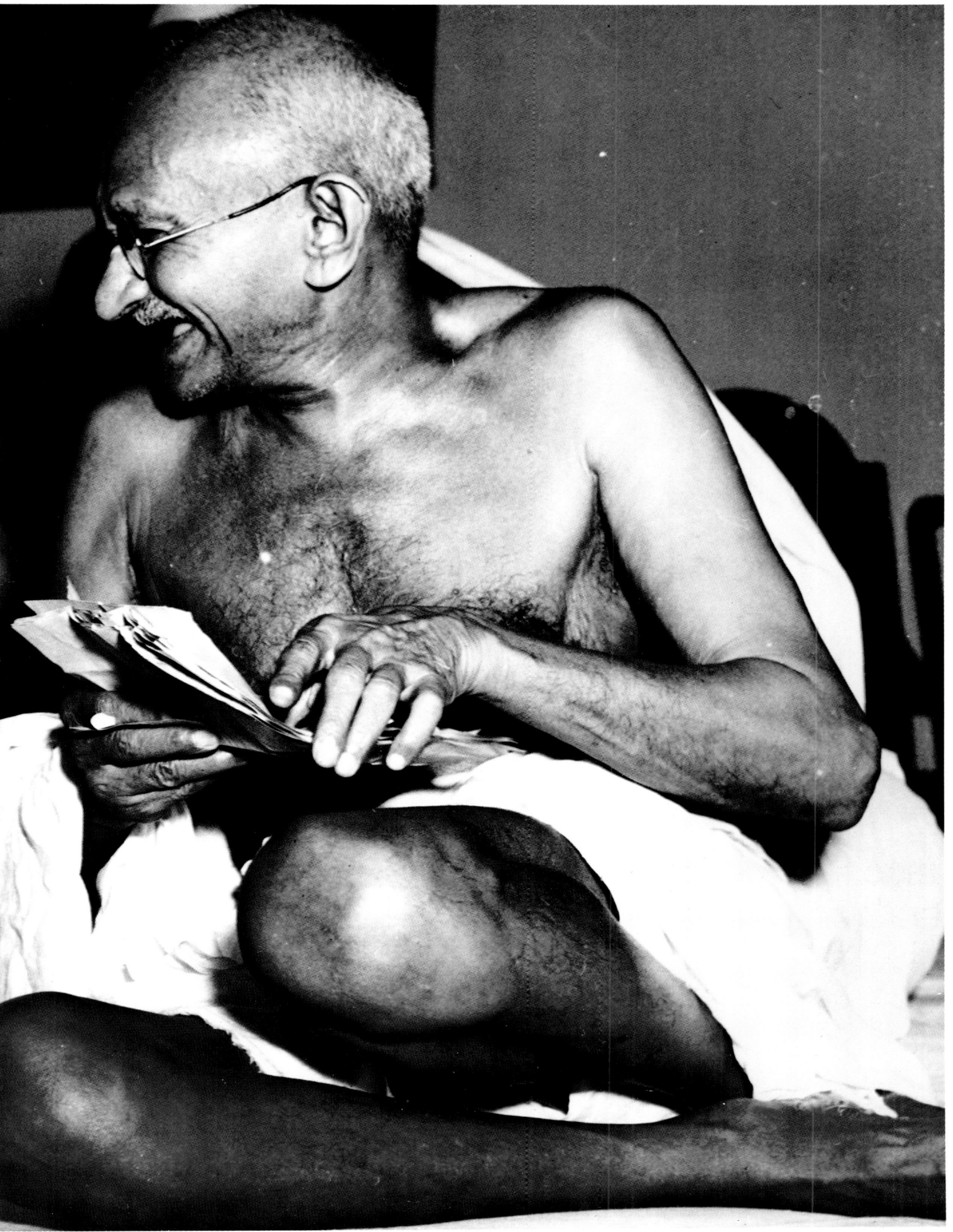

Royal Mourning

Britain's three queens — Queen Elizabeth II, the Dowager Queen Mary and Queen Mother Elizabeth — were among the mourners at Westminster Hall on Feb. 11, 1952, as the coffin of King George VI was brought in to lie in state.

The photograph was taken as the queens emerged from the hall and stood together for a moment, awaiting a coach. Ron Case, photographer for the Keystone photo service, said he saw them then "not as queens, but as grieving women."

Setting the Standard

It seemed almost impossible at the time; a barrier that humans would never overcome. To run a mile in less than four minutes?

Roger Bannister, studying to be a doctor, had been training to meet that challenge. On May 6, 1954, he believed he was ready.

Running for the Amateur Athletic Association against Oxford University in Oxford, the British athlete got Chris Chataway to pace him — and hit the tape with a 3:59.4. clocking. Photographer Chris Brasher recorded the historic moment.

Bannister was the first to do it. His feat seemed to deflate whatever psychological barrier there was, too, as others then set their sights on his standard and plucked seconds off his mile time. Thirty years later, the world record was 3:47.33.

MMmmmmm

The beauty of a butterfly . . .

A voluptuous blonde fantasy, eternal and ephemeral . . .

Marilyn Monroe.

"Half child," many said of her—"but not the half that shows."

That was the sweet sexuality, the pulchritudinous paradox of the movie Marilyn, born Norma Jean Baker, an orphan, in Los Angeles in 1926. It was an image enhanced by her film roles and promulgated by her publicists.

No tangible image of her is better known than this one.

AP photographer Matty Zimmerman was among those gathered in the early hours of a September morning in Manhattan in 1954, when she was filming "Seven Year Itch."

A gust through the sidewalk grating . . . a childish grasp at modesty while immodesty reigned—and the fantasy was frozen forever.

The forlorn star died at the age of 36, a suicide.

"The beauty of a butterfly's wing, the beauty of all things," it has been written, *"is . . . sheer delightful waste to be enjoyed in its own high right."*

"Seeing" the President

"He has a wonderful smile."

Helen Keller, who could neither see nor hear, still experienced the well-known grin of President Dwight Eisenhower.

AP photographer Charles P. Gorry took the picture during Miss Keller's visit to the White House in November 1953.

Men and the Sea

It is an ancient, if unwritten, law of the sea: the captain stays with his ship.

Capt. Kurt Carlsen was determined not to break that tradition of responsibility and for two weeks at the start of 1952, the world fought the battle of the sea with him.

Carlsen captained the freighter Flying Enterprise. It ran into heavy seas off the south coast of England, forcing the evacuation of the crew of 40 and 10 passengers on Dec. 28, 1951. Carlsen remained, hoping he could help bring the freighter to port.

On Jan. 4, he was joined by Kenneth Dancy, first mate of the British tug Turmoil, which passed a towline to the Enterprise the next day.

Photos, taken from The Associated Press chartered tug Englishman, showed Carlsen and Dancy waving to well-wishers as the Flying Enterprise was towed 300 miles in rough water.

Then, the line snapped. The Enterprise went down 35 miles from the Cornish coast, on Jan. 10.

Carlsen and Dancy were rescued just 45 minutes before the ship sank.

Down to an Ocean Grave

The fog was thicker than usual that night of July 25, 1956. A thick veil seemed to mantle the sleek Italian liner Andrea Doria, as it passed some 45 miles south of Nantucket, Mass.

Eight days out of Genoa, Italy, the ship was headed for New York, some 200 miles away. Outbound, just five miles from her, was the Swedish liner Stockholm.

At 11:20 that night, the Stockholm's bow, heavily reinforced against possible ice in northern Atlantic waters, tore a jagged hole in the starboard side of the Andrea Doria.

The first large swell sent tons of water pouring through the gap. Almost immediately, the Andrea Doria began to list.

She sent out the distress call: "We are bending . . . impossible . . . put lifeboats at sea . . . send immediate assistance . . . lifeboats."

The French liner Ile de France was among those that sped to the scene. As the fog lifted, the Ile de France was able to help in the rescue of nearly 1,700 survivors of the collision. Fifty-one lives were lost.

In the light of morning, the pride of the Italian merchant fleet, the three-year-old Andrea Doria, sank in the Atlantic. A burst of foam and bubbles surged up as she went under.

The Pulitzer Prize-winning serial photograph of the sinking was made by Harry A. Trask of the Boston Traveler.

Hula Hoopla

It was only a plastic ring, maybe three feet around. But it became an international mania.

Hula hoops they were called, probably because the gyrations needed to keep them moving — without hands — resembled the Hawaiian hula dance.

The fad of the Fifties outdid goldfish-swallowing, telephone booth-stuffing or flagpole-sitting as a challenging inanity.

Kids stretched their imaginations to find different ways to twirl the hoop around.

This picture shows the results of youthful creative genius. Gathered in a parking lot to compete for prizes on the television show "Art Linkletter's House Party" in 1958, these tots and teens spun the hoops around their hips, necks, knees and ankles — some dancing on one leg or tap-dancing at the same time.

Adults used them for calisthenics; spectators wondered about the suggestiveness of it on some hips.

Manufacturers cheered, too.

Rites of Spring

It happens every spring.

Panting young men on campus "raid" the women's dorms and sorority houses for souvenirs of how the other half lives. They come away with inside information in the form of frilly lingerie.

This undercover affair took place at Vanderbilt in 1952.

Imprisoned Photographer

AP photographer Frank "Pappy" Noel had seen a great deal of war action in his work.

In 1942, while covering the Pacific theater, Noel's boat was torpedoed off Singapore and he and 27 other survivors spent five days in a lifeboat before reaching land. (He won a Pulitzer Prize for a photo taken during the ordeal; see page 19.)

He carried his camera through Europe for the remainder of World War II, then covered the Palestinian war in 1948. . . .

Then the Korean War.

Captured by the Communist Chinese, Noel spent 32 months in a prison camp at Pyokdong in North Korea near the Yalu River. The picture of the bewhiskered photographer was received in Paris from a Peking picture source late in 1951. He displayed his AP picture envelope for identification.

He shot a series of pictures of his fellow POWs, with the consent of his captors. This one was taken in February 1952.

Korea

It was like too many similar pictures of too many similar wars. The U.S. Signal Corps photo by Sfc. Al Chang in the Haktong-Ni area of Korea in August 1950 pictured a grieving U.S. infantryman whose buddy had been killed in action being comforted by another soldier. In the background, a corpsman methodically filled out casualty tags.

Four months later, at Pyongkang, North Korea, it was the chaos and confusion of evacuation, of flight out of fear. Hordes of Communist Chinese troops had entered the war as allies of North Korea and pressed south.

AP staff photographer Max Desfor made the dramatic Pulitzer Prize-winning picture of fleeing refugees crawling over the shattered skeleton of a vehicular bridge across the icy Taedong River on Dec. 4. Thousands of them made the perilous trek over the jagged girders, carrying their bundled belongings with them.

Elvis

"Love Me Tender."
"Don't Be Cruel."
"Heartbreak Hotel."

Elvis Aron Presley was an immediate sensation as an entertainer beginning in the mid-1950s. His stage gyrations put new meaning into rock 'n' roll and turned teen-age girls into screaming hysterics.

The singer was not quite as popular with their parents, however, who were shocked by the tight pants, bucking hips and dangling guitar of "Elvis the Pelvis." At first, television producers refused to show him below the waist on screen.

But his popularity and huge success, whether with live performances, records or films, never waned.

The Hole Sole

Adlai Stevenson, then governor of Illinois, was a Democratic presidential hopeful in 1952. After winning the nomination from Sen. Estes Kefauver of Tennessee, he set out to make 100 speeches over 30,000 miles.

The wear and tear shows on his shoe.

On Sept. 2, Labor Day, in Flint, Mich., Stevenson put the slipshod foot up for a rest while making last minute revisions on his speech and was caught by Flint Journal photographer Bill Gallagher.

When the photo won a Pulitzer Prize, Stevenson wired Gallagher:

"Glad to hear you won with a hole in one."

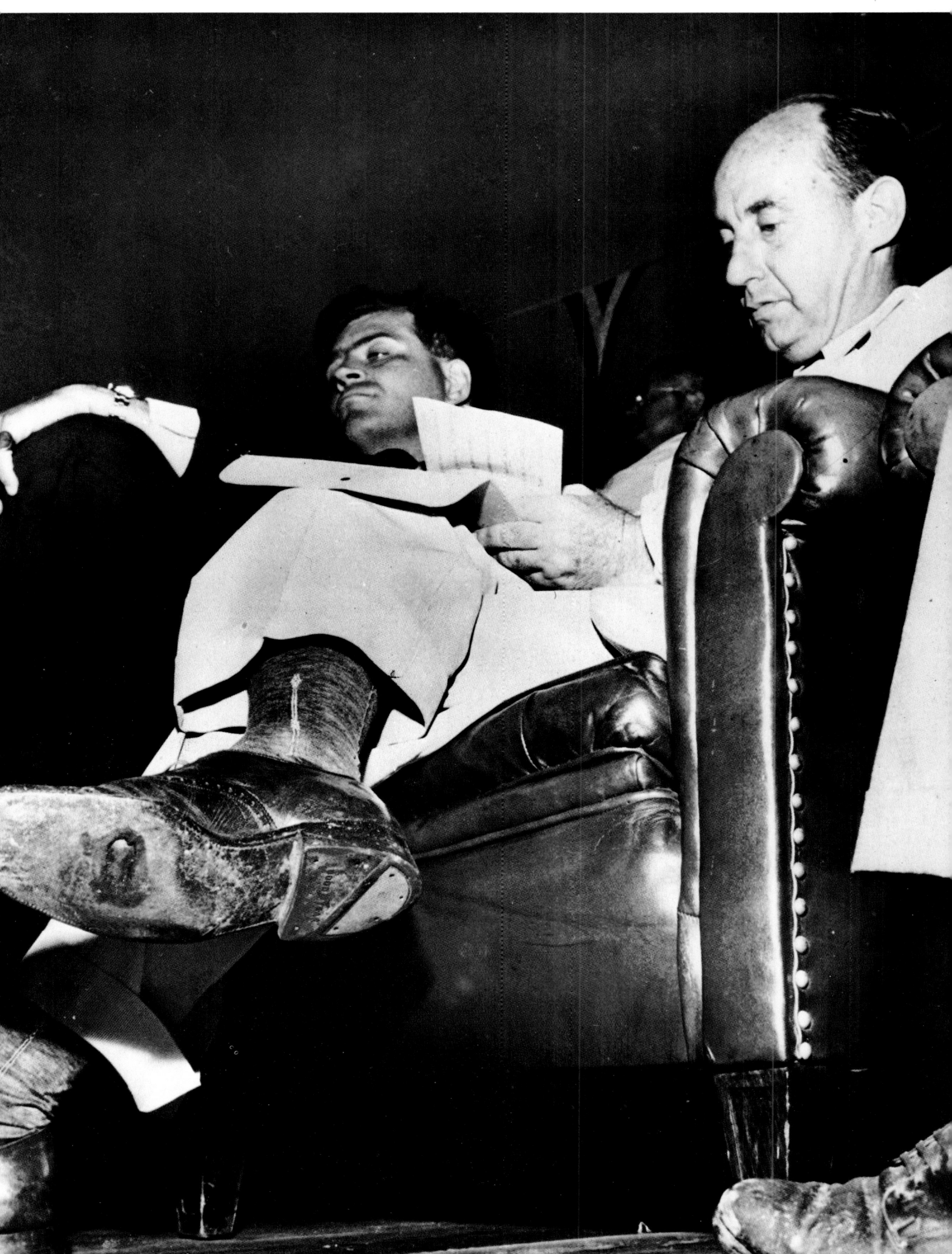

Beach Tragedy

There is nothing more chief lifeguard F.M. Cox can do but offer his sympathy. At his feet is the limp body of 7-year-old Patricia Thomas. She and her 9-year-old brother Raymond had wandered away from a picnic ground on the shore of Hansen Dam Reservoir in Roscoe, Calif., the previous day, July 27, 1947.

Cox had just recovered Patricia's body. Mrs. Thomas walked away in tears. Minutes later, searchers found Raymond's body.

The dramatic picture was taken by Paul Calvert of the Los Angeles Times.

Men Overboard

When these sailors were forced to abandon their fishing boat Hiroshima Maru in the Pacific and head for the Hawaii shore, photographer Warren Roll was there to take the unusual picture.

They carried with them their personal gear, secured to glass fish floats.

V for Winnie

"I have nothing to offer but blood, toil, tears and sweat."

"We shall defend our island whatever the cost may be. We shall fight on the beaches, we shall fight on the landing grounds, we shall fight in the fields and in the streets, we shall fight in the hills, we shall never surrender."

"Never in the field of human conflict was so much owed by so many to so few."

"I have never promised anything but blood, toil, tears and sweat. Now, however, we have a new experience. We have victory. The bright gleam has caught the helmets of our soldiers and warmed and cheered all our hearts."

The encouraging eloquence came from Prime Minister Winston Churchill, who took the helm in Britain's darkest hour and steered a course to victory over Nazi Germany.

He became the symbol of the determined spirit of Britain in wartime, of the courage of the British in the face of their gravest dangers. In the dark days of the blitz, he would visit bomb-scarred sections and make a V-for-Victory sign that he made a trademark.

He died soon after his 90th birthday, in January 1965.

His coffin was carried down the steps of St. Paul's Cathedral followed by members of his family.

Belfast Bombing

Gun battles . . . bombings . . . car explosions . . . riots . . . slaughter and destruction. Violence is an everyday fact of life and death in Northern Ireland.

There's been no stopping it since August 1969, when British troops were called out to head off Protestant-Catholic clashes that came close to civil war.

At the core of the violence is the Irish Republican Army, battling to wrest control of

allies sworn to resist any move to make the province a Catholic-dominated republic.

The moment of explosion of one such bombing in Belfast is caught in this dramatic picture, which won the World Press Photo award in 1980 for Bienfait/Achtin Press.

Leap to Freedom

The barbed wire and wall separating East and West Berlin was up only three days when 19-year-old Conrad Schumann reported for duty as an East German border guard on Aug. 15, 1961.

When the other guards turned their backs, the young soldier made his break to the West to join his family, which had fled earlier.

The photograph was taken by Peter Leibing, of the Hamburg picture agency Contipress, who had been tipped by police that an East German guard might be coming over. He waited at the Bernauer Strasse and was ready when Schumann made his move. No shots were fired. On the West side of the barricade, police brought up a small truck and opened the back door for the ride to the police station — and freedom.

In the first year of the Wall, more than 50,000 people escaped East Germany. As the wall has been "improved," strengthened with steel and cement, with explosives and attack dogs, with guards ordered to shoot anyone who tries to flee, the number of those who have succeeded has diminished considerably.

Invasion Defiance

Czechoslovakia's dream of democratic reform turned suddenly to nightmare. The Czechs woke up the morning of Aug. 21, 1968, to find that some 70,000 heavily armed soldiers of the Soviet Union and other Communist bloc nations had invaded their country, with tanks and modern weapons.

Older Czechs felt suddenly dismayed and wept. Youth was defiant. Many tried to block the advancing tanks with their bodies. They shook their fists, set tanks afire, waved bloody flags and shouted, "Russian murderers go home."

But the defiance was futile.

At School's Door

"I had high hopes and aspirations. I thought we would just go in and be accepted," recalled Thelma Jean Mothershead Wair, one of the nine blacks who tried to integrate Little Rock's Central High School in September 1957.

"Bad? No, it was . . . ugly is a better word. It was an ugly time."

For three weeks, National Guardsmen acting under orders of Arkansas Gov. Orval Faubus blocked the black youths at the school's door. When the Guardsmen were called off, whites surrounded the nine youths and shouted abuse.

Finally, President Eisenhower ordered an end to the obstruction. He sent the Army's 1st Airborne Division to Little Rock to make sure Central High would desegregate peacefully.

In this photograph, black students Richard Richardson (left) and Harold Smith are surrounded by whites.

Dogged Demonstrators

The civil rights confrontation in the spring of 1963 focused on Birmingham, Ala.

There, it was the Rev. Martin Luther King's announced cause, "Break Birmingham and we break the South," against Police Commissioner Eugene "Bull" Connor and anti-parade ordinances.

For days, the demonstrators defied police and accepted imprisonment. By May 3, 800 were in jail.

On May 6, with youngsters like the 17-year-old in this photograph joining the march, the demonstrators refused orders to stop. The police used firehoses. The march and the singing went on. Then came the dogs.

Five blacks were hurt; two policemen bruised; 250 more blacks in jail.

The photographs, by AP's Bill Hudson, caught the attention of the world.

Mississippi March

James H. Meredith, the black who enrolled at the University of Mississippi in 1962 despite its segregation policy, undertook another personal challenge in June 1966.

He decided to march 225 miles from Memphis, Tenn., to Jackson, Miss., "to tear down the fear that grips Negroes in Mississippi" and "to encourage the 450,000 Negroes remaining unregistered in Mississippi. . . ."

On the second day of the journey, he was just south of Hernando, Miss., when, at about 4:15 p.m., a hefty white man wearing dark glasses and brandishing a shotgun appeared out of the trees along the road.

The shotgun roared once, then twice more. AP photographer Jack Thornell, who had been leap-frogging the march from its start, reacted instinctively to the sounds.

Meredith fell to the ground in agony. He turned to spot his hunter in the foliage.

In a Memphis hospital, doctors found gunshot in his head, back and legs. The wounds were not serious.

Aubrey James Norvell was arrested and charged with assault with intent to murder.

Meredith finished his journey—with 16,000 companions—22 days after he started it.

Thornell won a Pulitzer for the photographs.

Race Riots

The roots of rebellion are deep and raw when race is involved.

In the United States in the 1960s, blacks frustrated by bigotry, intolerance and inequality took their anger to the streets.

Often they were met by anger.

The clashes staggered a nation that prided itself on its heritage of democracy and equality.

Urban areas, where the lacks of living were more focused and more frustrating, were turned into battlefields. Cities burned as emotions erupted; riot police fought demonstrators from Jackson, Miss., to Detroit, Mich. Summers of violence darkened streets from Newark, N.J., to Chicago, Ill.

Death and destruction littered the path to civil rights.

Samurai Assassin

Inejiro Asanuma, 61-year-old chairman of the Japan's Socialist Party, was speaking at a political forum in Kibiya Hall in Tokyo on Oct. 12, 1960—about fair campaign practices—when it happened.

A slender 17-year-old named Otoya Yamaguchi charged up to the stage and stabbed Asanuma twice just under the heart with a foot-long samurai sword. The fanatical right-wing student was immediately grabbed by members of the audience and wrestled to the ground.

Yasushi Nagao of the Mainichi Newspapers of Toyko caught the moment as Asanuma reached out in an effort to ward off the second thrust. Asanuma was dead by the time he reached the hospital operating table.

Police said Yamaguchi told them he had plotted the assassination for three days and had no accomplice. They said he believed Asanuma was a traitor trying to sell Japan to the Communists.

Less than a month later, the young assassin hanged himself in his cell.

(Nagao won the Pulitzer Prize in news photography for the dramatic picture.)

Campus Crisis

Campus revolt became a matter of national concern in 1969. The University of Wisconsin. San Francisco State College. City College of New York. Harvard.

Then Cornell.

On April 19, to dramatize charges of racism on campus and a request for an autonomous Afro-American College, 250 black students took over the student union building, Willard Straight Hall.

Some members of the Students for a Democratic Society formed a protective picket line. Some fraternity members tried to cross it and were beaten back. There were reports that armed whites would invade the hall. Rifles and shotguns were smuggled in to the blacks in the building.

After 34 hours, Cornell President James Perkins agreed to amnesty and the blacks agreed to come out.

AP photographer Steve Starr was ready when the rebellious students emerged carrying their weapons and looking more like wartime guerrillas. The shocking picture of battle dress on the nation's campuses won a Pulitzer Prize.

Comrades in Arms

The United Nations General Assembly session in September 1960 provided the occasion for these two new political friends to embrace in public. The bearded Cuban Premier Fidel Castro got a Russian bear hug from Soviet Premier Nikita Khrushchev on the floor of the Assembly. AP photographer Marty Lederhandler was there to mark the jovial moment.

Presidential Partners

It's April 1961. The thorny topic probably is about Cuba.

They share the presidential burden in a private moment.

AP photographer Paul Vathis saw the new, young President John F. Kennedy —just three months in office—walk down the stone path at Camp David, Md., with 70-year-old former President Dwight D. Eisenhower.

"They look so lonely," Vathis recalled.

The picture earned him the Pulitzer Prize.

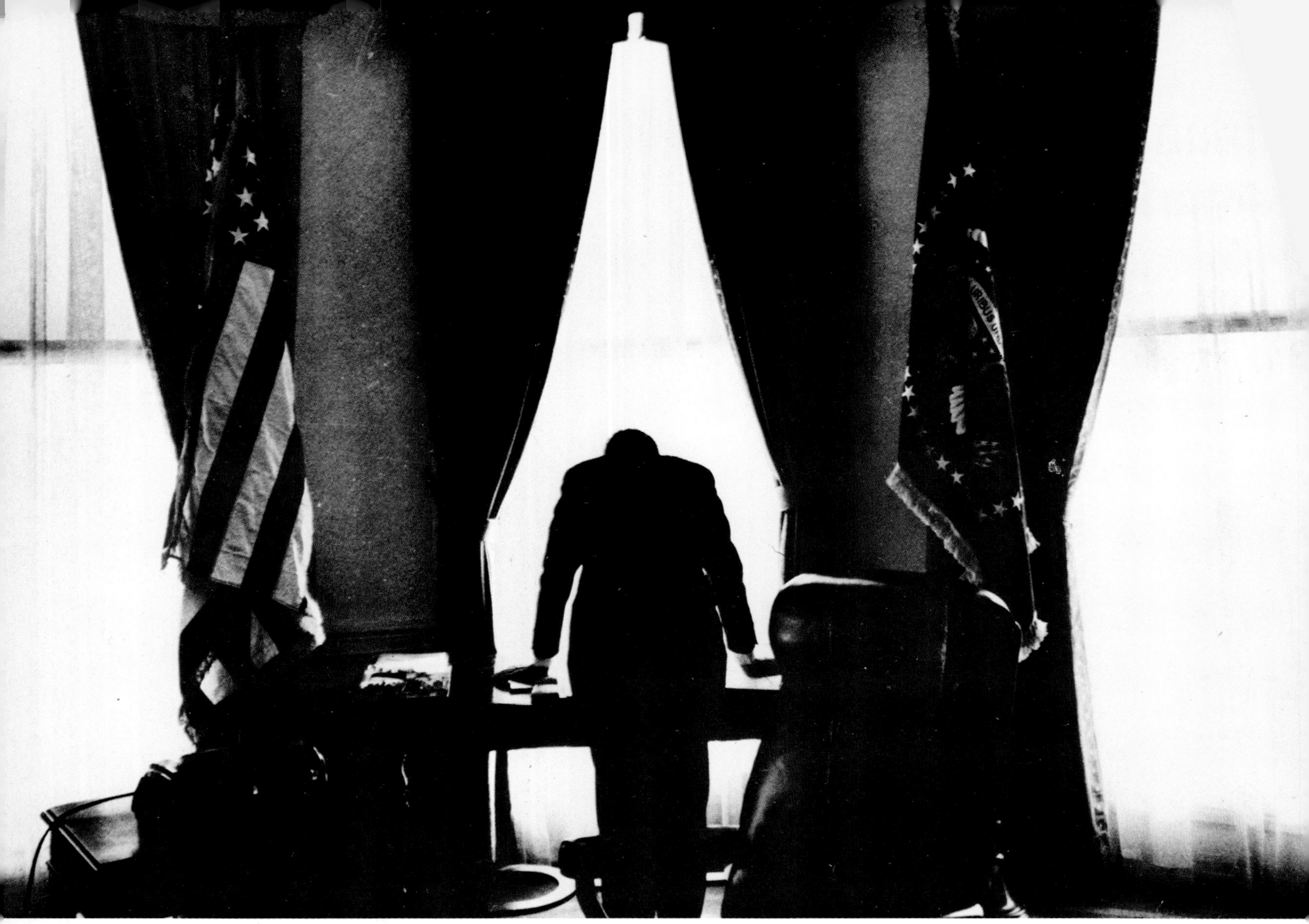

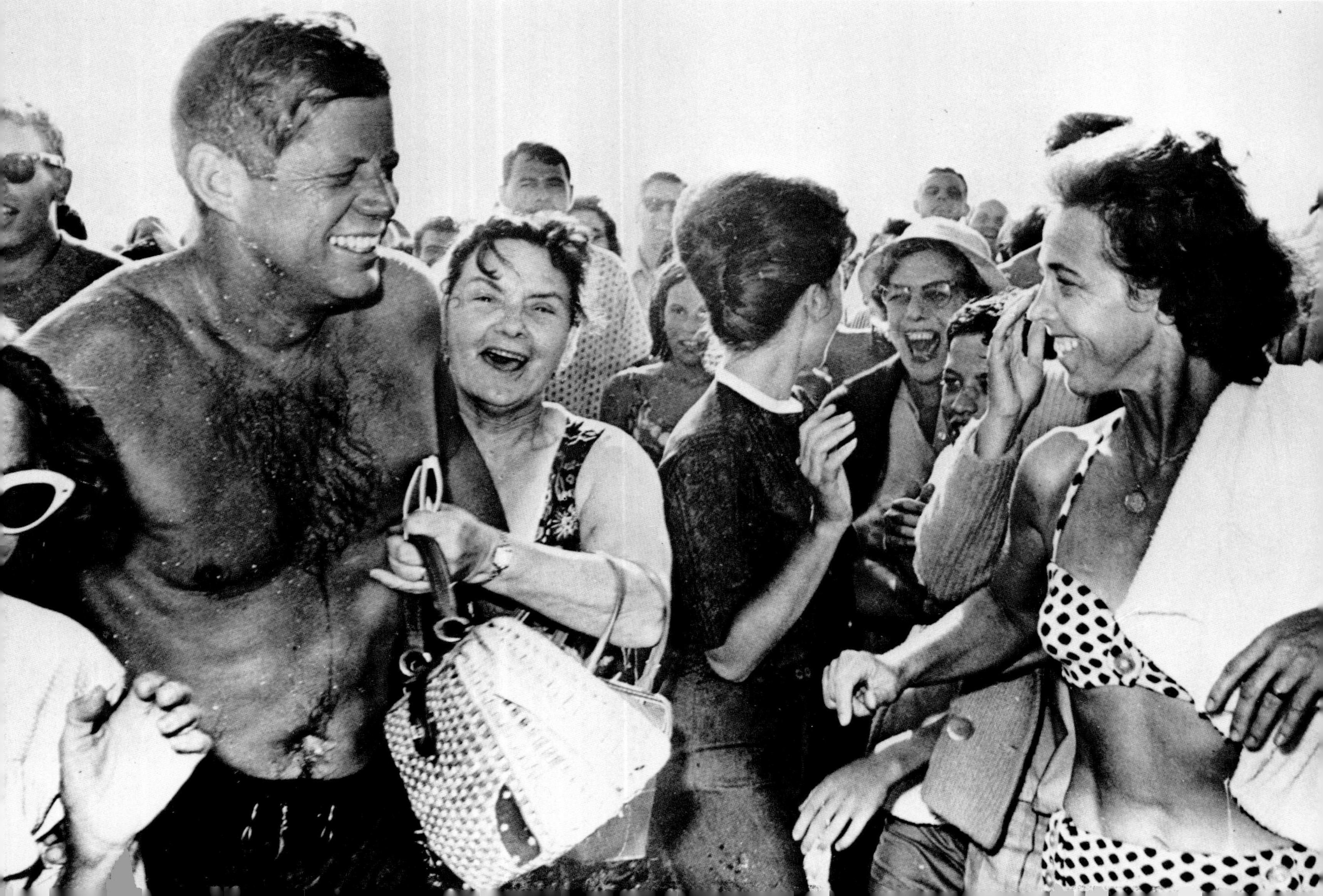

Triumph and Tragedy

"The measure of a man's success," once said the wealthy patriarch of the Kennedys, Joseph P. Kennedy, "is not the money he's made; it's the kind of family he's raised."

First and foremost, the Kennedys were a family: a family of money, a family of intellect, a family of elan and elegance and ease that came from a life of privilege.

One son, John Fitzgerald Kennedy, became president of the United States, and brought to the nation a new spirit of hope, a spirit brimming with confidence and dedicated to progress.

"Let the word go forth from this time and place . . . that the torch has been passed to a new generation of Americans. . . ."

John Kennedy's hopes at his inauguration were echoed by the visions of poet Robert Frost on that January inaugural day in the nation's capital in 1961. Americans, Frost said, were about to enter a "golden age of poetry and power, of which the noonday's the beginning hour."

John Kennedy was a brother, too. He worked closely with the younger Robert Kennedy, whom he had named attorney general of the United States.

And John Kennedy was a father as well. "He'd rather have walked the beach with Caroline at the Cape than have met with Khrushchev in Vienna," said an old family friend.

And young John Jr. When he arrived and when he left, little John was there to see him.

FLASH
DALLAS—PRESIDENT KENNEDY DIED AT 1 P.M.

BULLETIN
DALLAS, NOV. 22 (AP)—PRESIDENT JOHN F.
KENNEDY, THIRTY-FIFTH PRESIDENT OF THE UNITED
STATES, WAS SHOT TO DEATH TODAY BY A HIDDEN
ASSASSIN ARMED WITH A HIGH-POWERED RIFLE.

The tragedy shocked and benumbed the nation. Television and print images recounted the horror. The motorcade . . . the "crack!" of a shot . . . the race to the hospital, in vain.

The blood-spattered widow, Jacqueline Kennedy . . . her grief veiled as she was handed the flag that covered the casket.

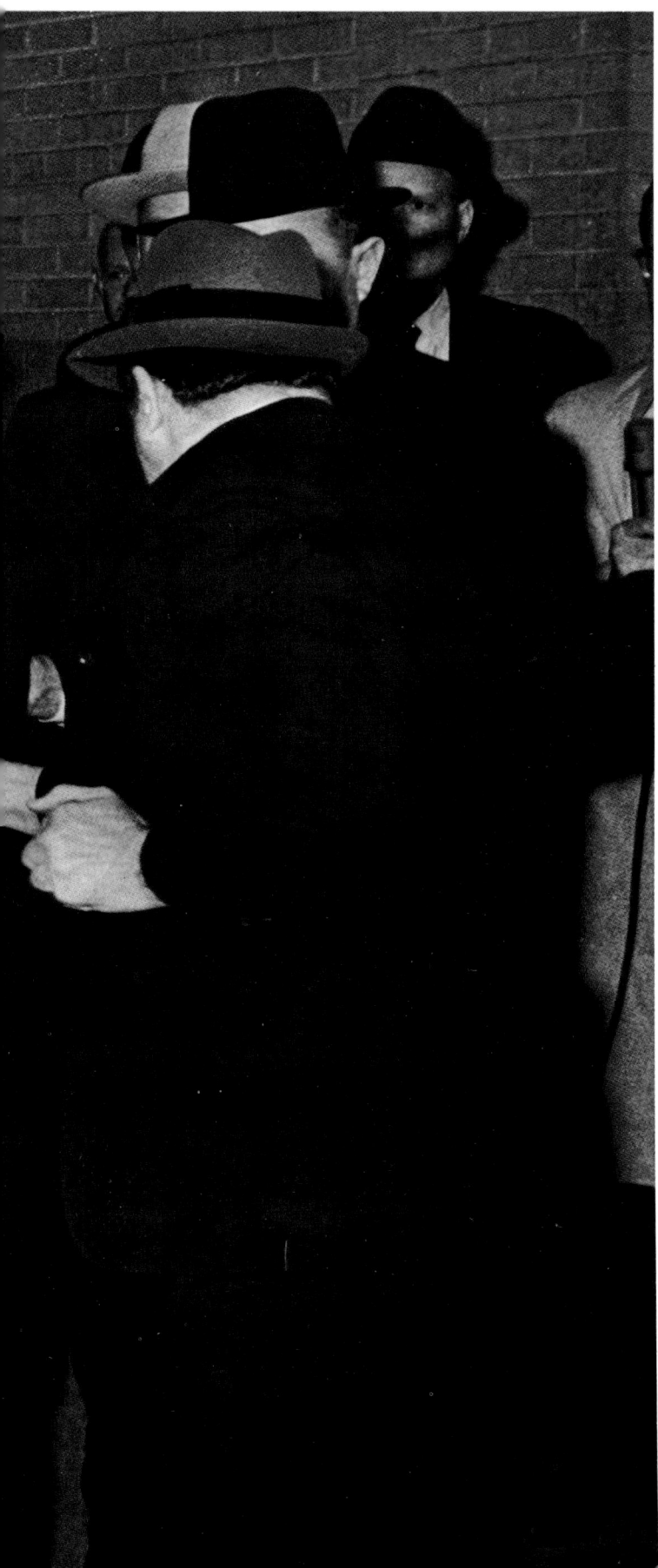

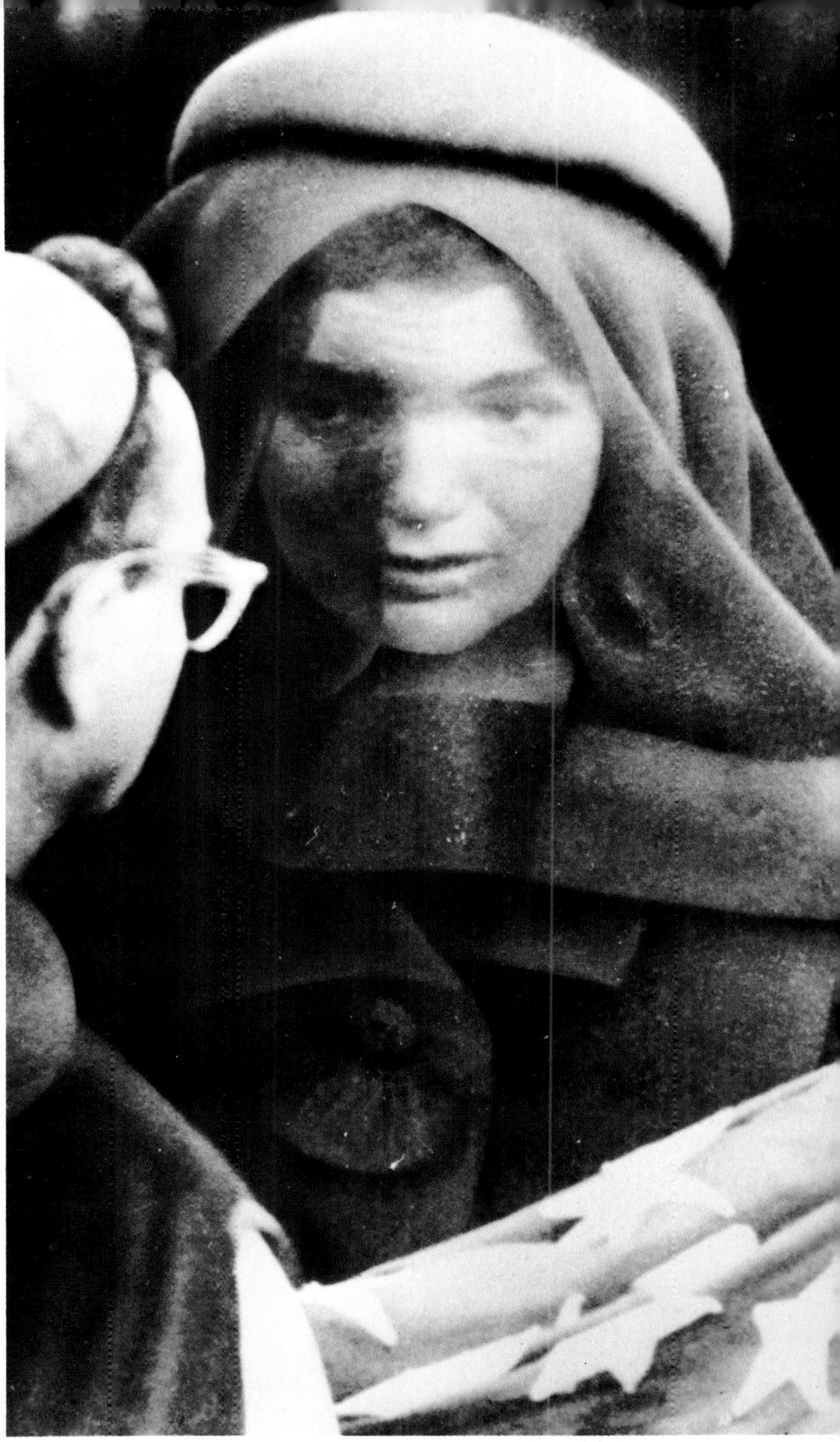

The shocks persisted.

BULLETIN
DALLAS, NOV. 24 (AP)—LEE HARVEY OSWALD, ACCUSED SLAYER OF PRESIDENT KENNEDY, WAS SHOT TODAY APPARENTLY IN THE STOMACH AS HE LEFT THE CITY HALL UNDER HEAVY GUARD EN ROUTE TO AN ARMORED CAR FOR TRANSFER TO THE CITY JAIL.

Shot by a local club owner named Jack Ruby. (Photo © Dallas Times-Herald, by Bob Jackson.)

And still the calamities would not stop.

Robert Kennedy, then a U.S. senator, campaigned for the presidential nomination in California in 1968. On June 5, after a primary election victory speech at the Ambassador Hotel—another assassin's bullet struck down a Kennedy.

Photographer Boris Yaro of the Los Angeles Times © was there barely moments after the shooting.

The triumphs . . . and the tragedies . . . of the Kennedys.

"Don't let it be forgot
"That once there was a spot
"For one brief, shining moment
"That was known as Camelot . . ."

King is Shot

The Rev. Martin Luther King Jr. had a dream: Equality. Blacks and whites together. He dreamed it could be accomplished without violence.

In April 1968, he was in Memphis, Tenn., supporting a garbage workers' strike for union recognition and higher pay. Ninety-eight percent of the strikers were black.

On April 3, King spoke at Mason Temple. He spoke about the violence he hoped to prevent. And he revealed that there had been threats against him.

"It really doesn't matter with me now," he said, "because I've been to the mountaintop, and I don't mind."

He was pictured that day on the balcony of the Lorraine Motel, with colleagues Hosea Williams (left), the Rev. Jesse Jackson, and on his other side, Ralph Abernathy.

It was on that balcony the next evening, April 4, when it happened just before 6 p.m. The crack of the rifle shot was flat and crisp.

Police quickly poured into the area when they heard of the shooting.

Joseph Louw, Public Broadcasting Laboratory assistant producer of a TV show on King's planned Poor People's March, was in a room two doors away. When he heard the shot, he rushed out and photographed King's aides as they yelled to police and pointed to where the shots came from. (Life magazine obtained his picture exclusively.)

Two months later, James Earl Ray was named as the killer. Investigations showed he was a lone assassin.

The Informal Presidency

President Lyndon Johnson was an "earthy" man, downright "down home" and friendly as any of the White House occupants.

In 1965, he hid nothing from reporters and photographers, including AP's Charles Gorry, who came to see him at Bethesda Naval Hospital after he had had an operation for a gall bladder and a kidney stone. He called them over to show them the incision.

At another time, he held up the ears of his dog, "Her," so photographers could take pictures. That's "Him" watching.

That one got him (the president) into some trouble with animal lovers, who objected to that kind of treatment from the chief of state.

Slight, of Hand

Words failed Vice President Nelson Rockefeller when student demonstrators heckled him during an appearance in Binghamton, N.Y., in 1976. He returned their rudeness in kind.

Robert Dole, then Republican vice presidential nominee, was in the background, but apparently didn't notice the sign language conversation.

AP photographer Don Black, however, was well aware of the digital demonstration.

The Ultimate Protest

In 1963, when this series of astounding photographs was taken, South Vietnam was rocked by inner religious-political turmoil culminating in events that shocked the world.

The minority Buddhist population had protested their treatment by the government of Ngo Dinh Diem, a Catholic anti-Communist who had become the republic's first president after the Geneva Agreement of 1954. For weeks, the Buddhists had been demonstrating against what they considered persecution by Saigon officials. After a government ban on flying the Buddhist flag at church pagodas, a demonstration in the city of Hue in May 8 had ended in the deaths of 11 civilians.

Now it was June 11. Saigon.

Malcolm Browne, then an Associated Press correspondent, received a tip to go to Phan Dinh Phung Street that morning. There, he found a growing crowd of Buddhist monks and nuns chanting the ancient Buddhist prayers in unison.

At exactly 9 a.m. it stopped.

Unfurling banners in English and Vietnamese, the 250 Buddhists formed two lines behind a gray sedan. The procession moved through the streets. At Le Van Duyet, a major Saigon boulevard, the car stopped. The marchers encircled it.

It was 9:20.

An old monk emerged from the car. Accompanied by two other monks, he walked to the center of the circle. There, he sat down on a broad pad and crossed his legs in the traditional lotus position. He was brought a clear plastic container. It held pink gasoline. A monk lifted it up, doused the seated monk's head and shoulders, soaking his saffron robe. He emptied the bottle and placed it next to the monk, Thich (Venerable) Quang Duc, 73 years old. Other monks lay in front of fire trucks nearby, to prevent them from moving.

It was 9:25.

Malcolm Browne was less than 20 feet away, shooting these pictures. He described the stunning horror that followed:

"I could see Quang Duc move his hands slightly in his lap, striking a match. In a flash, he was sitting in the center of a column of flame, which engulfed his entire body. A wail of horror rose from the monks and nuns, many of whom prostrated themselves in the direction of the flames.

"From time to time, a light breeze pulled the flames away from Quang Duc's face. His eyes were closed but his features were twisted in apparent pain. He remained upright, his hands folded in his lap, for nearly 10 minutes as the flesh burned from his head and body. The reek of gasoline smoke and burning flesh hung over the intersection like a pall.

"Finally, Quang Duc fell backward, his blackened legs kicking convulsively for a minute or two. Then he was still, and the flames gradually subsided . . ."

Malcolm Browne won a World Press Photo Award for his pictorial document of this grisly act of protest, the ultimate protest.

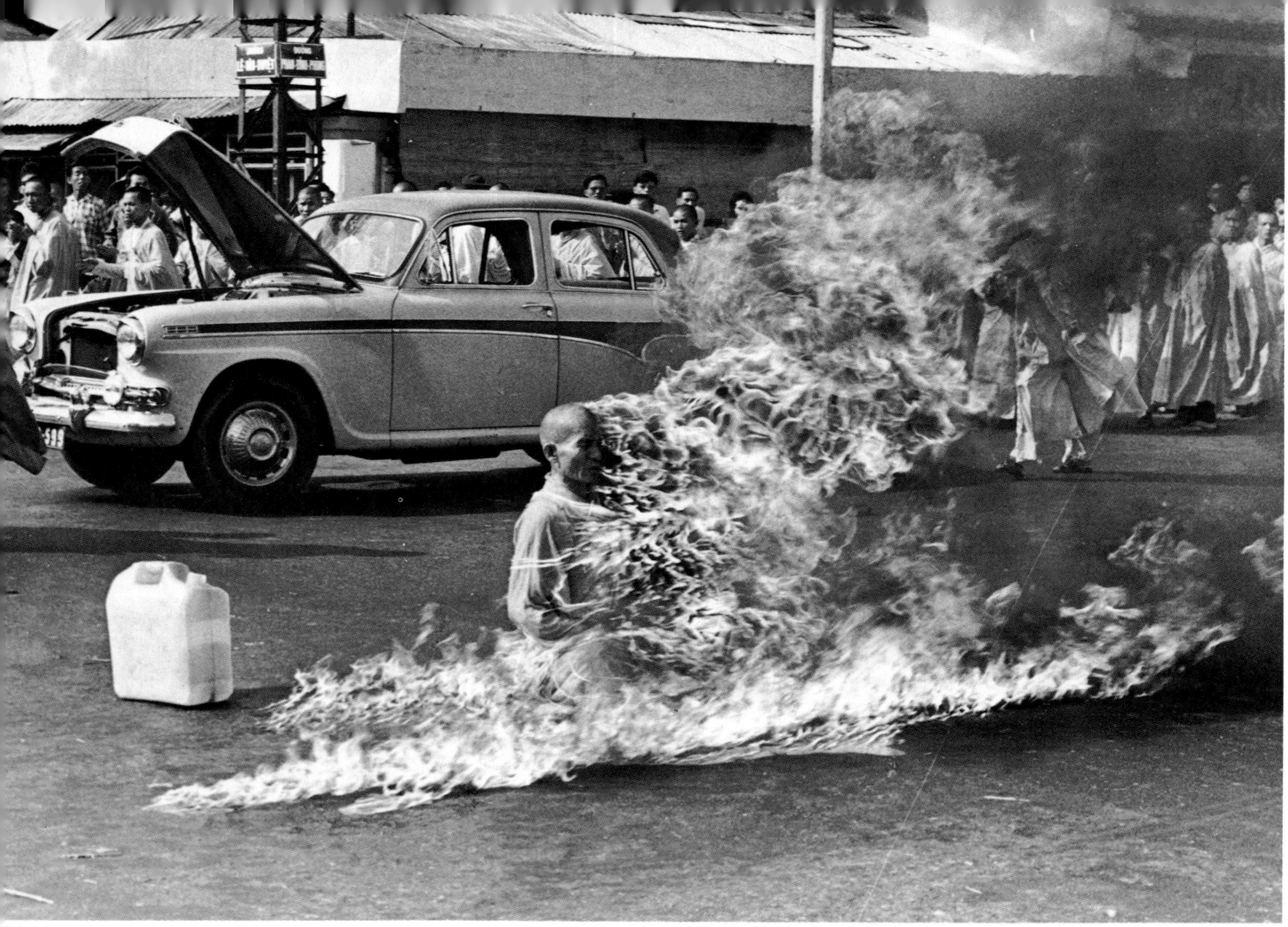

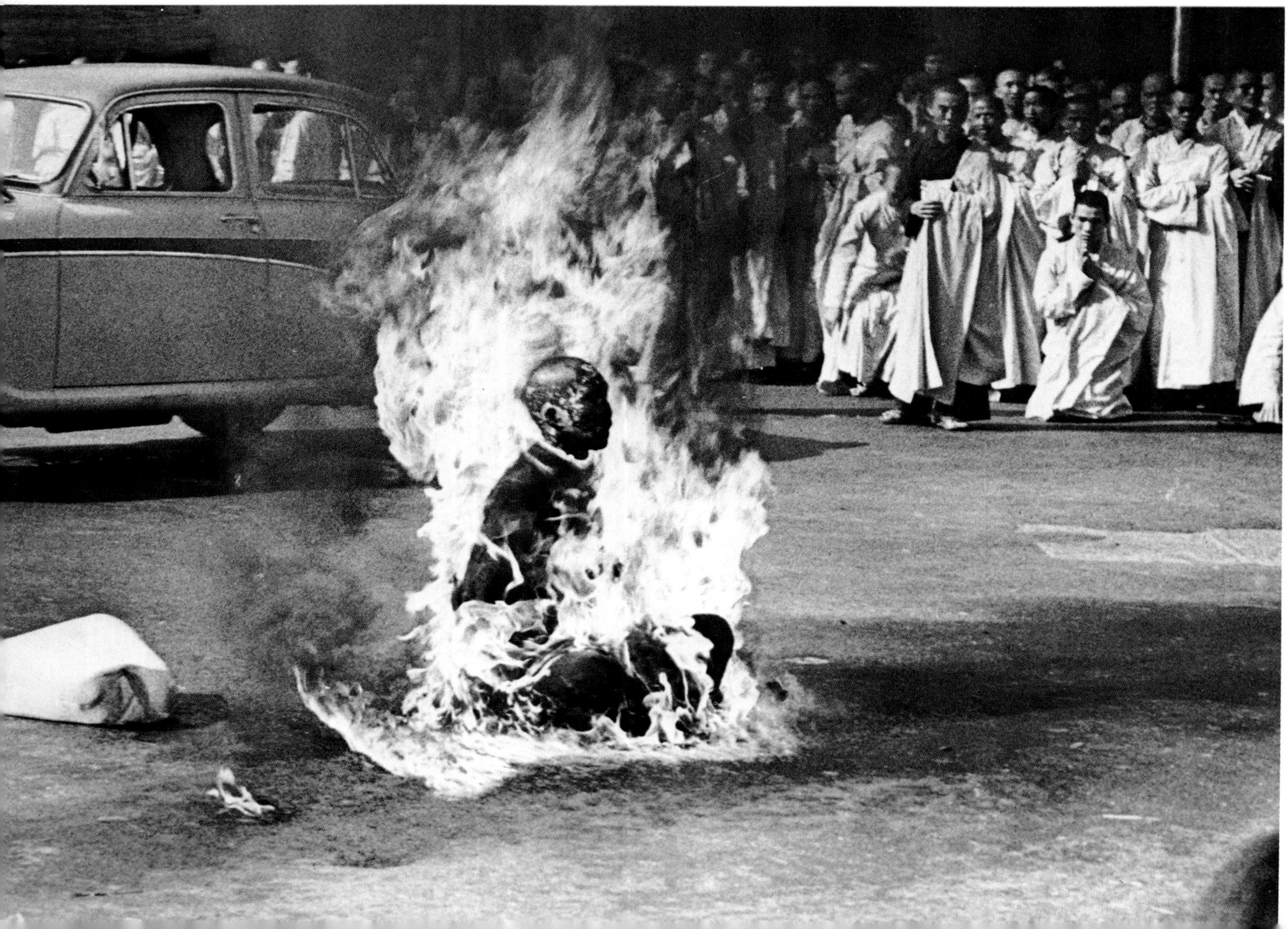

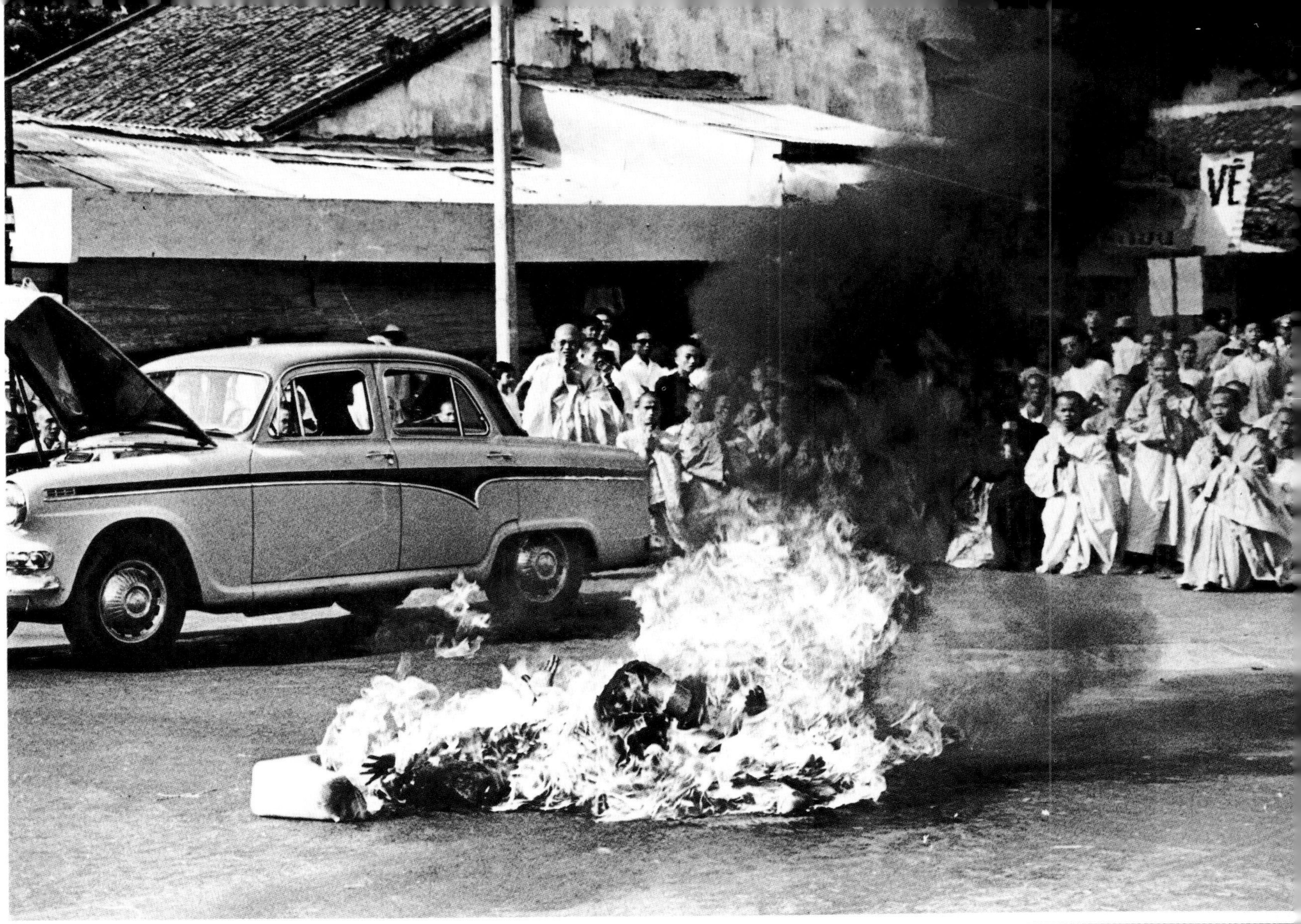
VÊ

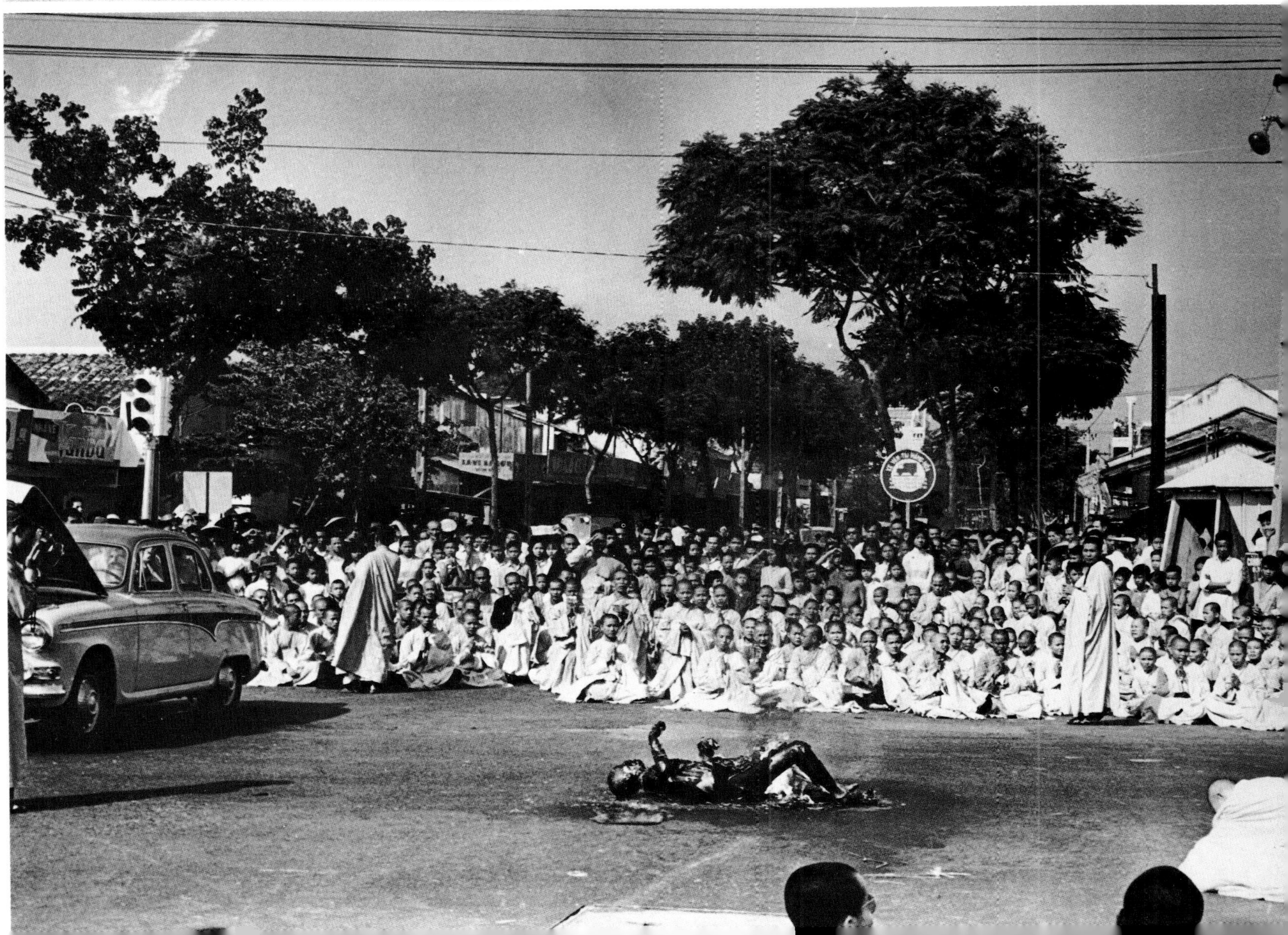

Naked Terror of War

The children; always the children.

Caught in the maelstrom of the mayhem of the Vietnam War, these terrified youngsters fled down Route 1, near Trang Bang in South Vietnam after an aerial napalm strike — an accidental one by an allied plane.

The 9-year-old girl in the center had ripped off her burning clothes as the children tried to outrace the horror.

South Vietnamese forces, coming down the road behind them, had called for air support that day, June 8, 1972. Two Skyraiders had attacked, but one dropped its flaming napalm on South Vietnamese troops and civilians instead.

Huynh Cong "Nick" Ut, an AP staff photographer, won the AP Managing Editors top photo prize for the scene of terror.

Faces of War in Vietnam

It was something of a quicksand war, a continuing conflict in which the more wriggles of peace, the more shouts of negotiated settlements, the more it seemed mired in death and devastation.

It was something of a picture war, with daily brutality and killing depicted on television news shows and in newspapers and magazines almost before the blood had dried and the bodies were buried.

In the end, it was a war that couldn't be "won."

It was Henri Huet's photo of Pfc. Medic Thomas Cole, his own head nearly half covered with bandages, as he tended his wounded buddies of the U S. 1st Cavalry Division in January 1966. On Cole's leg rested S/Sgt. Harrison Pell.

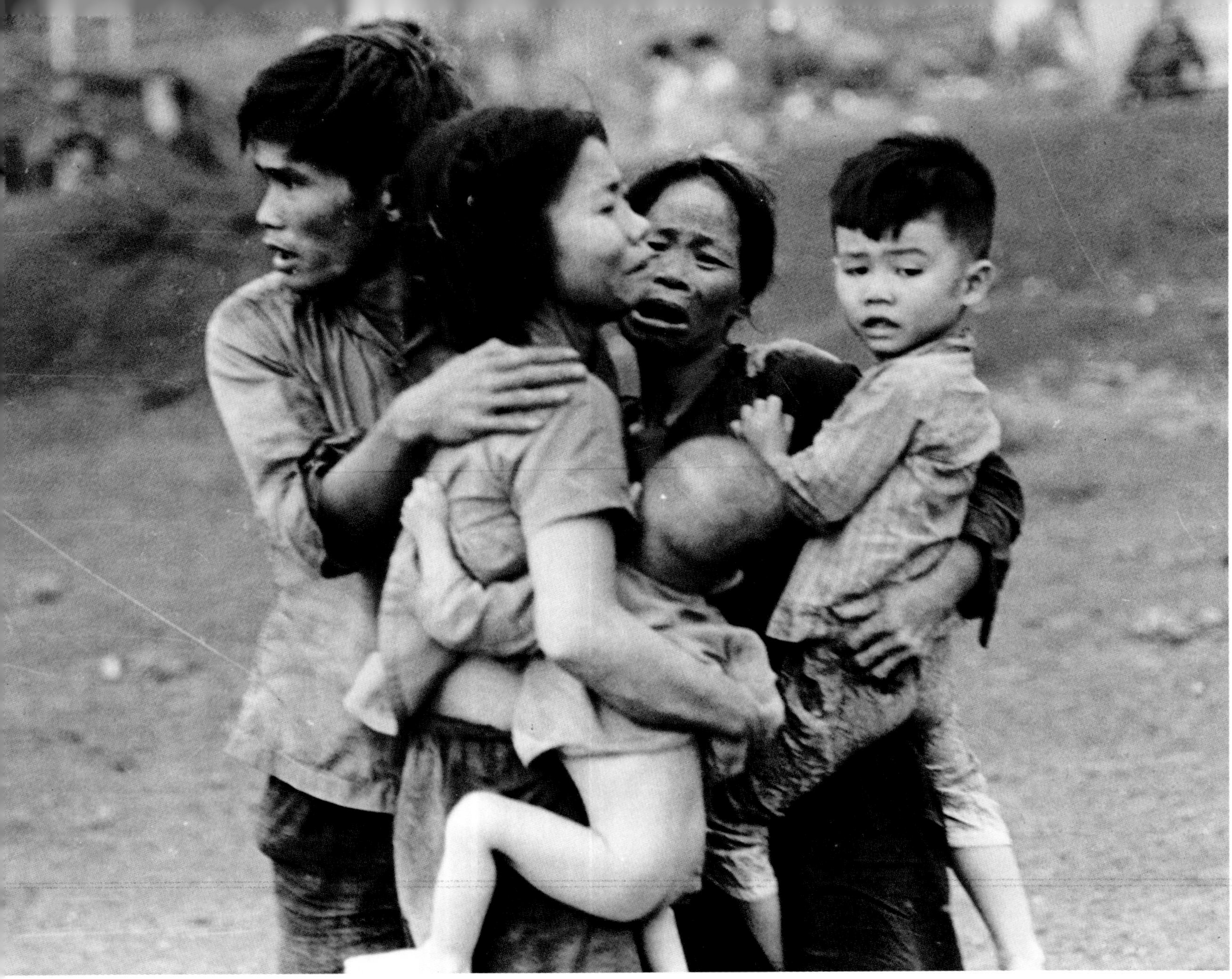

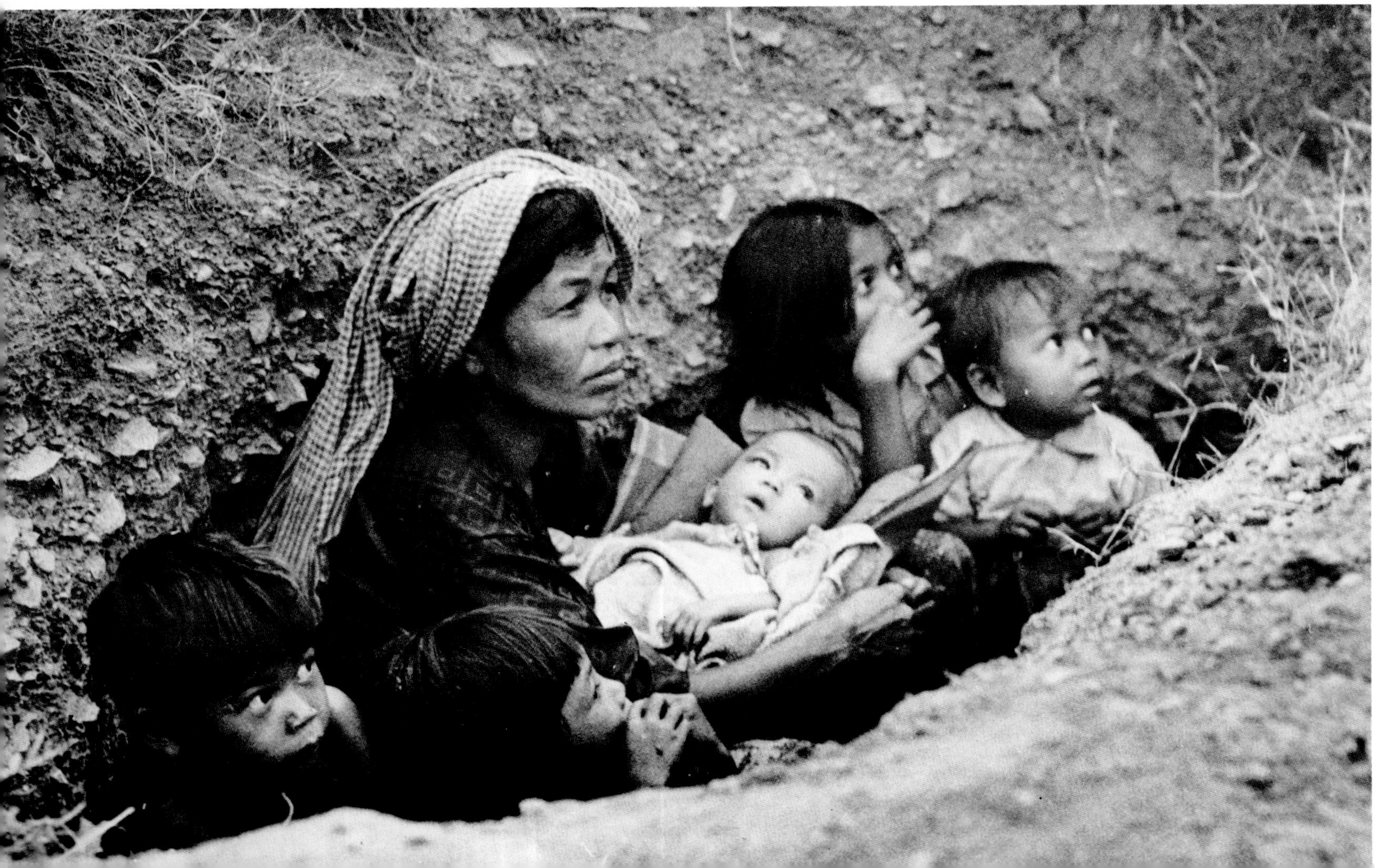

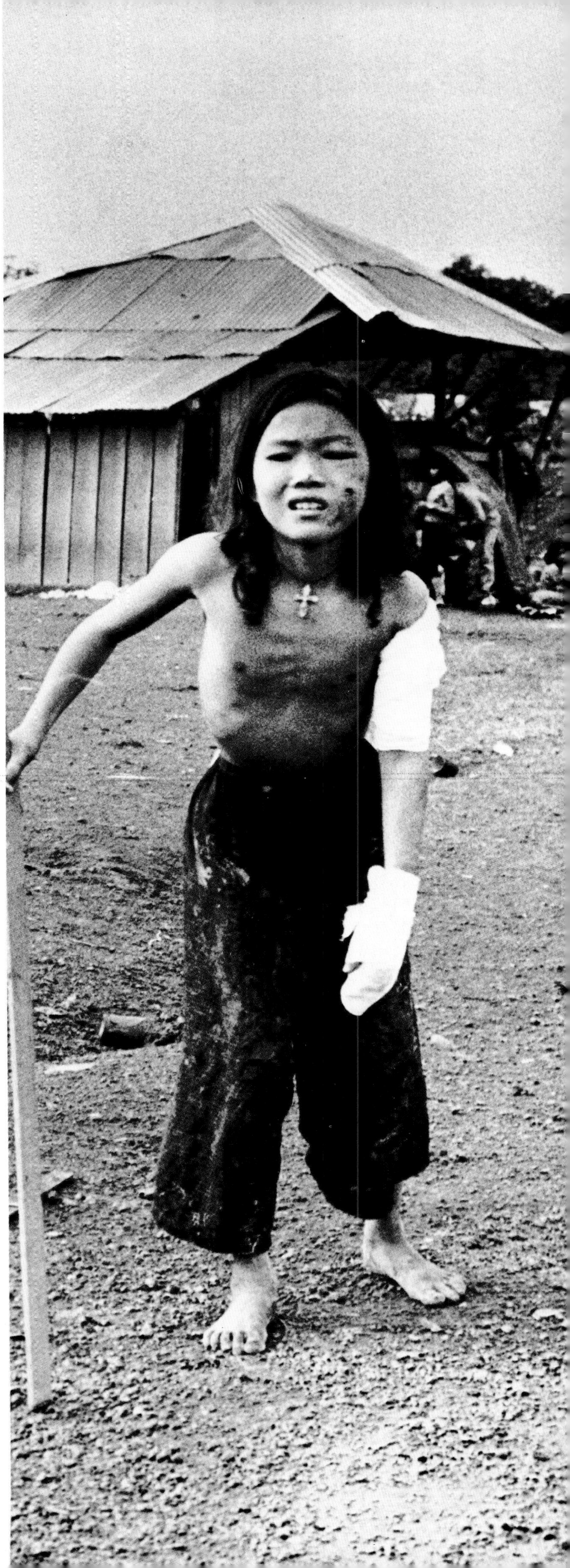

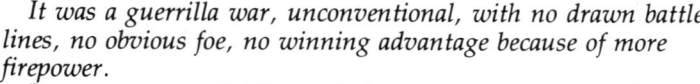

It was a guerrilla war, unconventional, with no drawn battle lines, no obvious foe, no winning advantage because of more firepower.

It was a war of attrition and the encounters were small, vicious, usually nonconclusive—and always bloody.

It was Horst Faas' photo of a South Vietnamese girl as she watched from behind a wooden fence when government troops marched through her village to check on Viet Cong activity in 1964. The child's village was set afire and the residents moved to a fortified area.

And it was the Cambodian woman with five children looking up apprehensively from a shallow bunker as shells fell around the capital at Phnom Penh in 1975.

The horror, the futility, the waste. . . .

In Faas' Pulitzer Prize-winning photographs like the one of a South Vietnamese Ranger who used the butt of his dagger to punish a South Vietnamese farmer for allegedly supplying government troops with wrong information on Communist guerrillas.

And his shot of the lone Vietnamese Ranger who sat on a tree stump amid his fallen comrades after a battle near Binh

Gia in December 1964. Or his photo of a Vietnamese soldier carrying a comrade who was wounded when a Viet Cong mine exploded under a truck convoy.

Faas also pictured civilian survivors, caught in a battle between Viet Cong and South Vietnamese forces near the jungle town of Dong Xoai in June 1965. The bodies of 150 civilians and 300 government troops were counted.

And, still, the children.

A cross dangling on her chest, her face taut with the pain of multiple wounds, a 12-year-old girl leaned on a stick and hobbled across a field strawn with battle rubble. Faas made the poignant picture as she struggled to reach an evacuation helicopter. Her mother and two brothers survived and claimed her in a Saigon hospital.

Other children were not as fortunate.

A father carried the body of his child, killed in a battle near the Cambodian border in March 1964, as South Vietnamese Rangers looked down from their armored personnel carrier.

In war, there are no winners.

Instant of Execution

The Viet Cong guerrilla, wearing civilian clothes and carrying a pistol, was captured near the Quang pagoda in Saigon during the Tet offensive, Feb. 1, 1968.

Identified as an officer, he was taken to the police chief, Nguyen Ngoc Loan.

Loan fired one shot into the head of the prisoner, whose hands were tied behind his back.

His victim grimaced at the impact and fell, dead.

Loan replaced his pistol in his holster.

"They killed many Americans and many of my people," Loan said.

The photograph, made on instinct by AP's Eddie Adams, won a Pulitzer Prize. It was also taken up by demonstrators who pointed to it as an example of their anti-Vietnam War attitudes.

It is, perhaps, the single most memorable of many memorable pictures of the war.

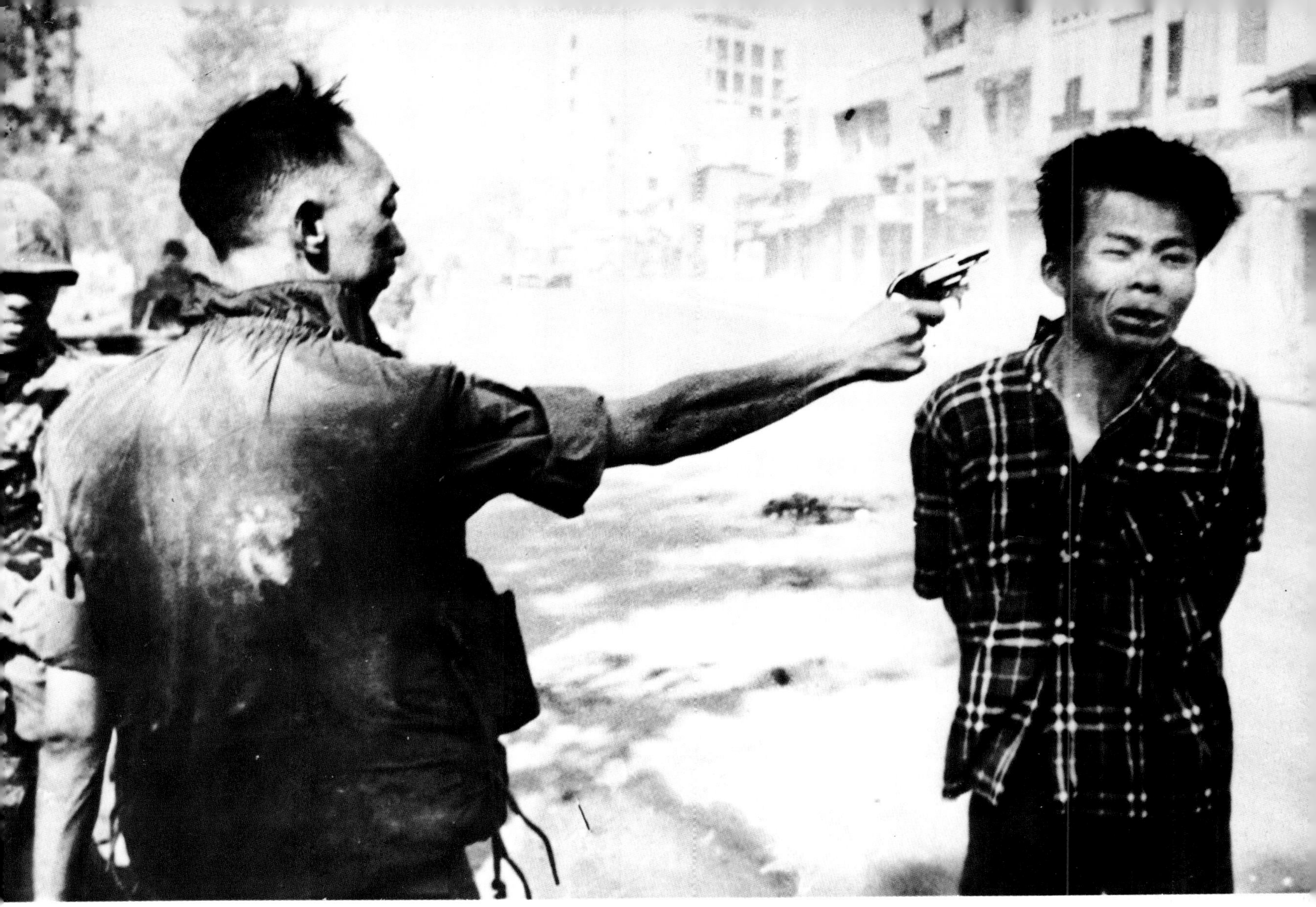

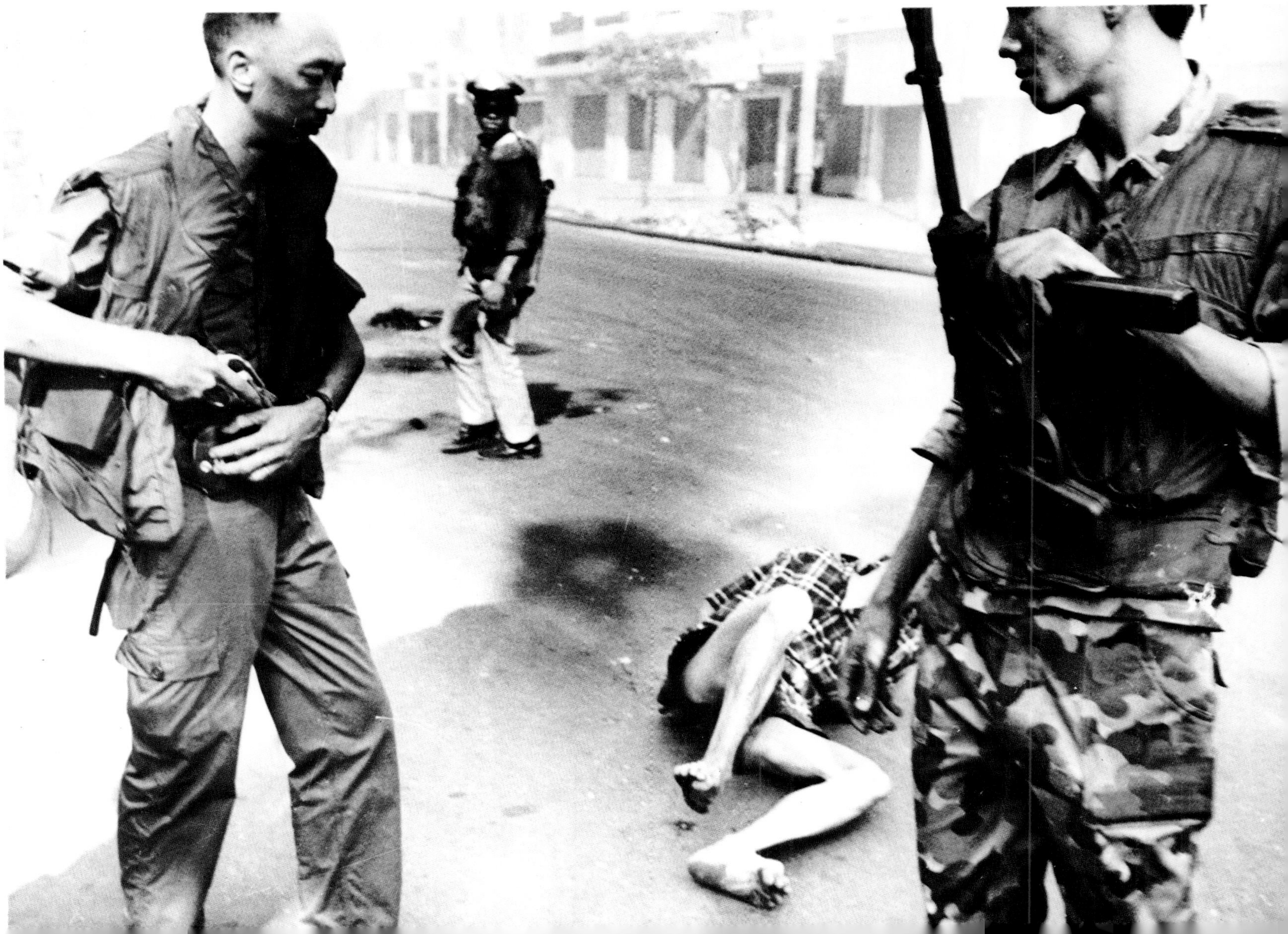

Divided Opinions

The effect of the Vietnam war was felt halfway around the world, as Americans split into factions of support or antiwar. Demonstrators on both sides let their opinions be known, coast to coast.

A march of protest against the war started out at the San Francisco waterfront and moved quietly and somberly seven miles to a rally in Golden Gate Park in November 1969.

On the other side of the nation—and the other side of the emotion—workers waved flags and patriotic signs to show their displeasure with antiwar sympathies of then-Mayor John Lindsay of New York.

Fatal Protest

The protest was against a South Vietnamese-United States attack into Cambodia — "Operation Total Victory" — an effort to deny the North Vietnamese sanctuary in that Asian nation.

Domestic reaction was swift; students in particular objected to any possible extension of a war that had already divided much of the nation.

On May 4, 1970, students at Kent State University rallied once again — despite the presence of National Guardsmen called in by Ohio Gov. James Rhodes — to declare their protest. Rocks were thrown. The Guardsmen reponded with tear gas. They aimed their guns. Suddenly, there were shots fired.

Four students were killed.

John Filo, then a student at Kent's journalism school, was on campus with a camera. He saw Jeffrey Miller lying in a pool of blood.

"Then this girl came up and knelt over the body and let out a God-awful scream," he remembered of the moment.

The telling picture of bloody protest at an American college was published in the © Valley Daily News, Tarentum, Pa., and earned a Pulitzer Prize for Filo.

Run Into
the Ground

Win? Place? No show?

Some trotters just seem to get their drivers into deeper and deeper trouble.

Actually, trainer-driver Robert Taylor had finished warming up his horse, Mateson, and was headed into a tunnel under the main track at the Lexington, Ky., Trots.

A few minutes later, they came out for a $700 race—and did show, placing third.

Nodding
to It

Those long, loquacious stately occasions can often be a bloody bore.

Even to those on the reviewing stand/speakers platform.

Photographer Ronald Bell, of Press Association Ltd., caught British Defense Minister Fred Mulley dozing off right next to Queen Elizabeth II.

Powerboat Perils

The thrills, the excitement, the danger. These may be the allures of powerboat racing, but it's not always fun and games.

This trio of photographs shows mishaps in the Rio Balsas in Mexico, Biscayne Bay, Fla., and rapids in Washington state.

The accidents killed one and injured several others, spectators and racers alike.

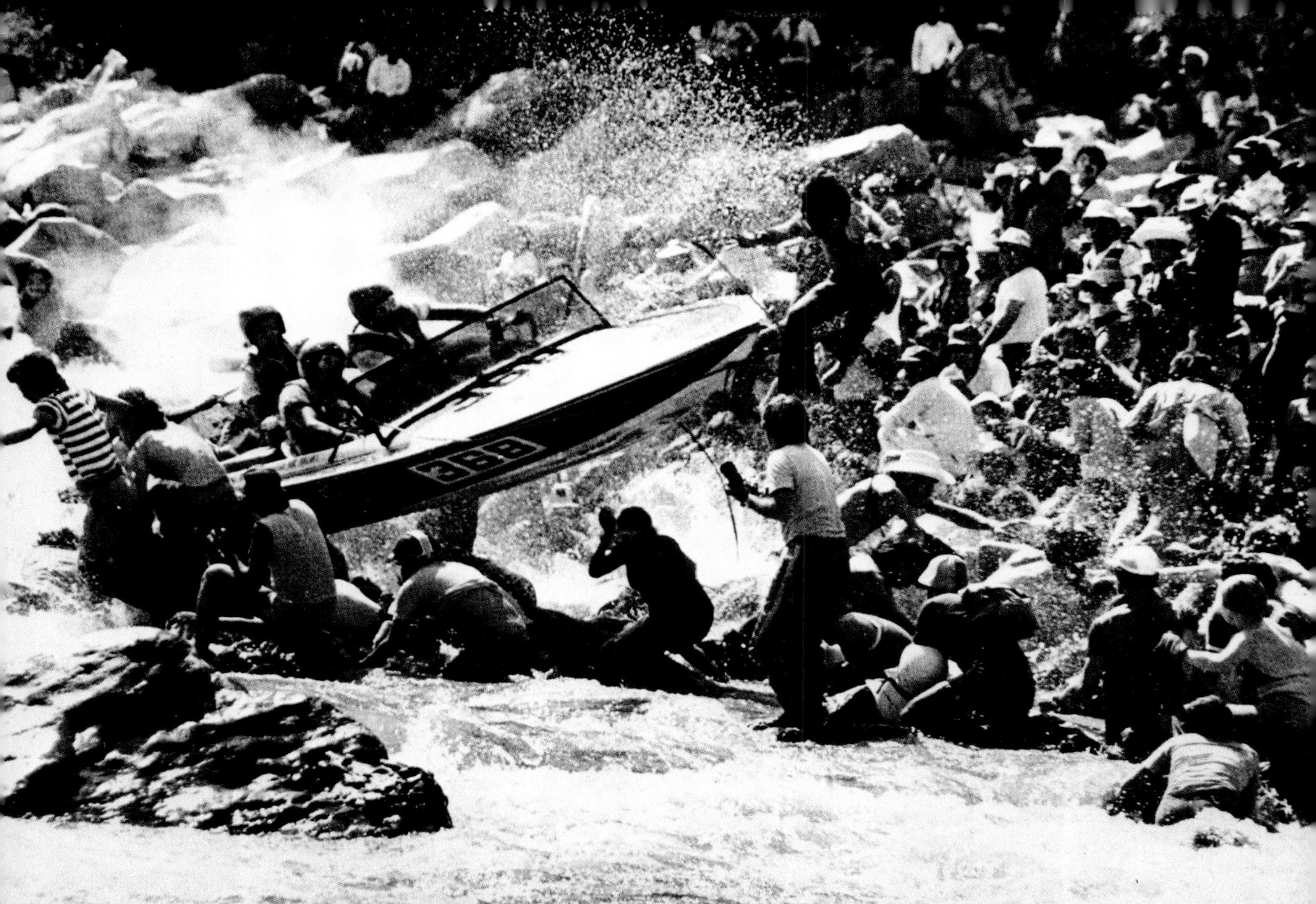
388
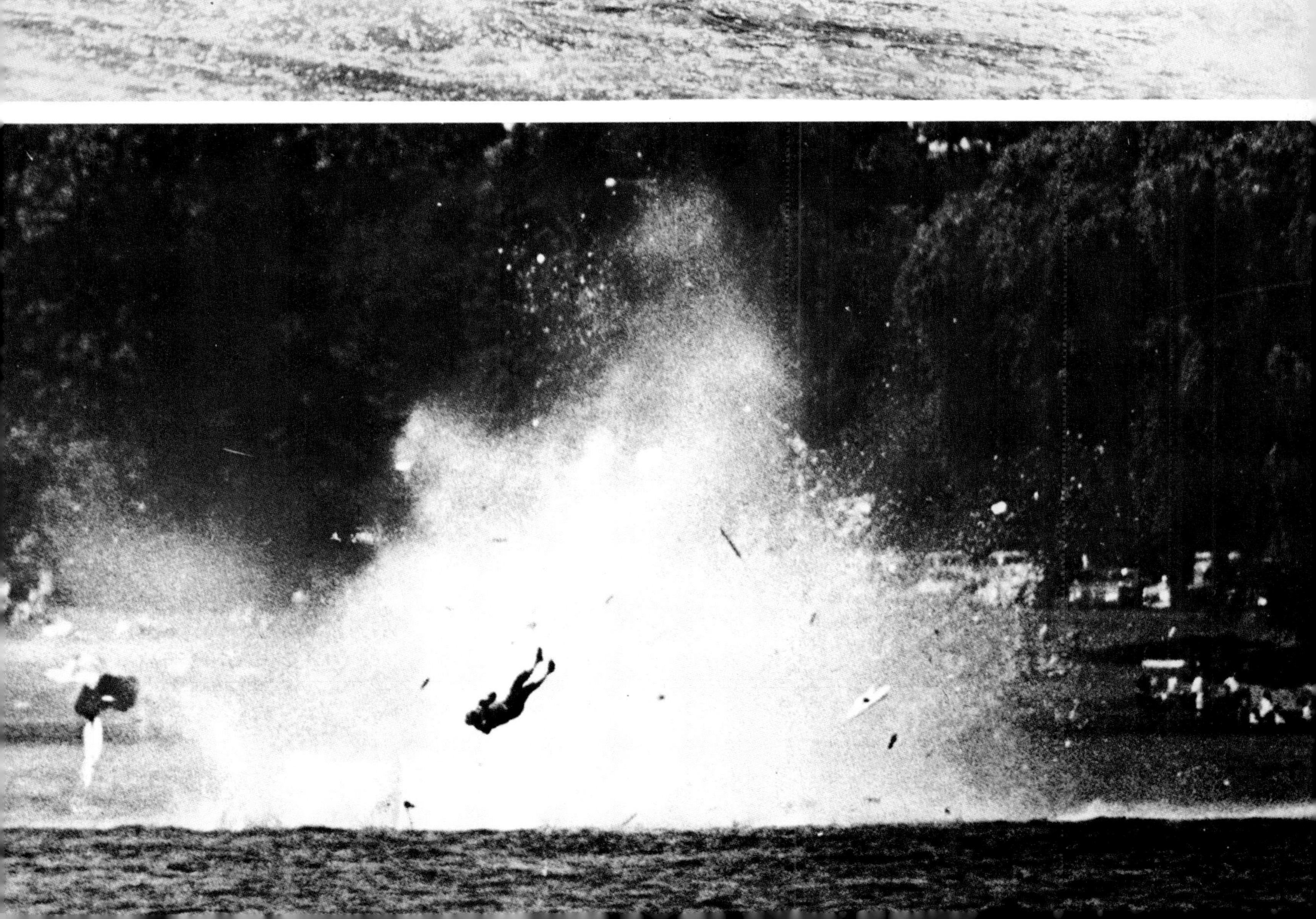

Stands Fall

The Indianapolis Speedway, home of the "500," has been the mecca for auto racing since its opening in 1911. During its long history, it has provided peril and poignancy, thrills, turmoil and tragedy for drivers, crews, families and spectators.

On May 30, 1960, there was tragedy even before the start. And it was not on the track.

Fans had been so anxious to see the race that temporary stands had to be built to accommodate the overflow. One-hundred-and-twenty-five of them paid $5 to $10 for a seat in the 30-foot temporary wood and aluminum scaffold.

As they jostled for the best view, the stands collapsed. J. Parke Randall, a racing fan, was shooting pictures for the Indianapolis News that day. He caught this sequence as the tower fell to the ground, some falling fans with their arms still upraised, debris and hats flying through the air.

Two men were killed and 70 others injured.

Quake Victims

The one who is alive is often the victim, too.

A weeping man carried his dying baby through the streets of Skopje, Yugoslavia, during an earthquake in July 1963. Hundreds of others were killed.

The photograph was taken by Sam Nocella of Willow Grove, Pa., who was with his wife in a Skopje hotel when the quake struck.

Death in Soweto

It began as a student protest against the compulsory use of the Afrikaan language in black schools on an equal basis with English. Most of the blacks in the segregated township of Soweto, outside Johannesburg, South Africa, regarded that Dutch-based language as the language of their oppressors.

About 2,000 black youths demonstrated their feelings on June 16, 1976. Police came with tear gas, batons, guns. The riot escalated and spread throughout the nation.

By the time it was over, at least 176—all but two of them blacks—were dead, including young Hector Petersen, carried here to a waiting car by one of the protesting students. Petersen's sister screamed in grief.

Fire Escape

When the fire, heat and smoke at the burning Taeyonkak Hotel in Seoul, South Korea, became too much to bear, some guests jumped in desperation, hoping a mattress would cushion their fall. Kim Dong-Joon, photographer for the Seoul Simbun newspaper, caught the moment when one man leaped from a ninth floor window; another, a floor below, was about to do the same.

Both died, among 155 victims that Christmas Day, 1971.

Freak Disaster

Allen White and his 13-year-old son Carl had just finished repairing a tractor tire at a gas station in Ellettsville, Ind.

As they inflated it, it exploded.

Anna White screamed as she discovered the bodies of her husband and son.

The picture was taken July 13, 1969, by Fred Sisson of the Bloomington (Ind.) Courier-Tribune seconds after the tire exploded.

Subzero Scene

Sunrise over Lake Michigan.

Nature awakens. Ducks fly out of the backlighted clouds of mist. Subzero temperatures turn the lake into a steaming, ultra-cold cauldron.

Rolling Prairie

There is a sense of mankind's continuity, a link with his past, in these serene, seemingly endless rolling prairies. In this photograph by John Filo, the Konza Prairie in central Kansas, unmarked by modern mechanisms, appears much as it probably did centuries ago.

Fiery Demonstrations

The fire of protest has heated many a demonstration over the years.

In 1969, Japanese students demonstrated against the war in Vietnam and for more autonomy for themselves. They took over part of Kyoto University, blocked gates, barricaded streets, overturned cars and set them afire. Riot police charged in against a hail of student firebombs.

The fire caught two students. Photographer Katsui Aoi of Asahi Shimbun caught them in his camera lens as the pair ran, and then rolled on the ground to extinguish the flames.

In 1978, at the new Tokyo International Airport, the scene was strikingly similar. A demonstrator's clothing caught fire during a violent clash between protestors and riot police. The demonstrator was engulfed in flames when he tried to hurl a blazing gas bottle at police.

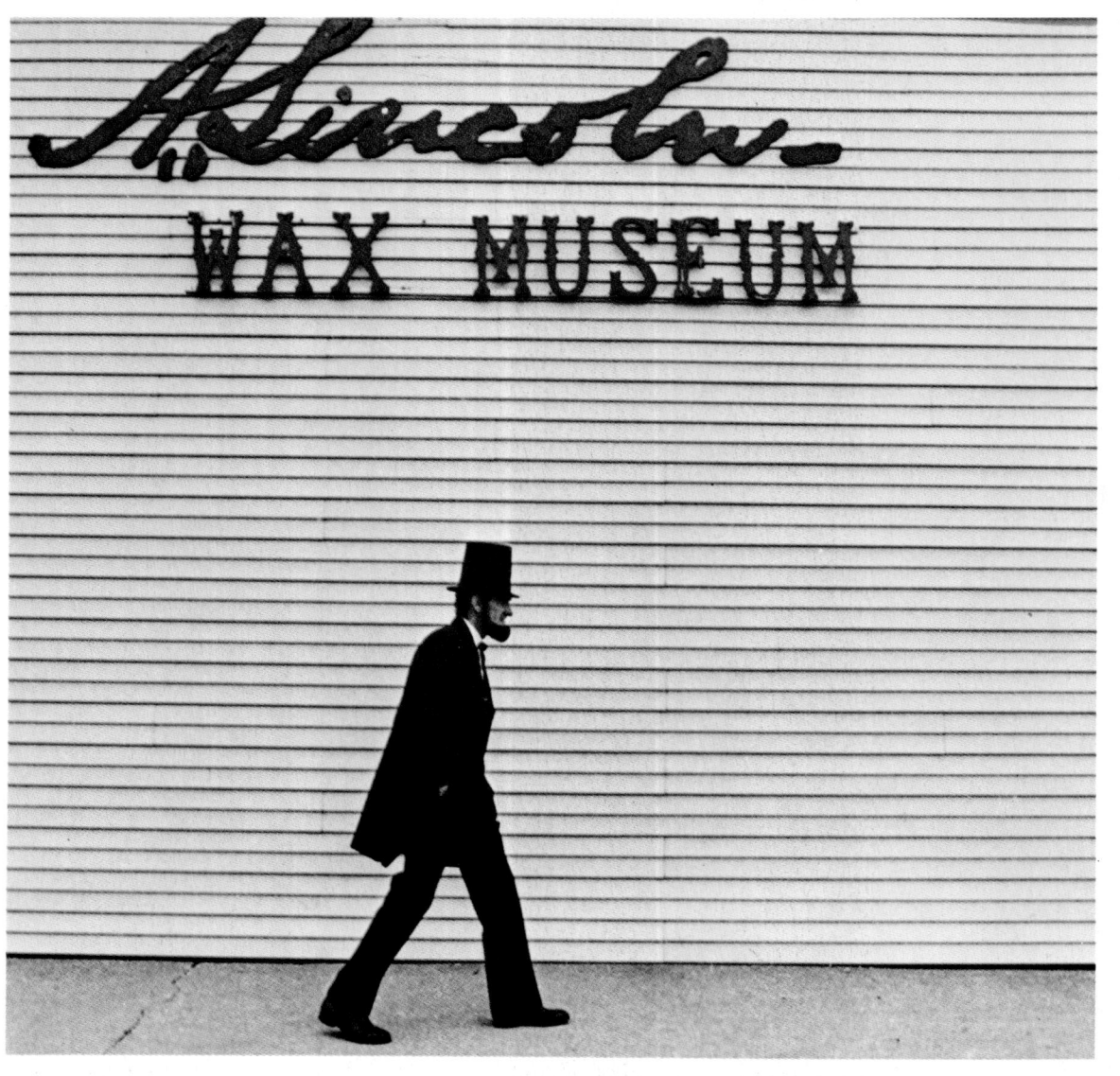

Waxwalks

It is Springfield, Ill., where Abraham Lincoln first practiced law. And it surely does look like Abe himself walking around town.

Except that it's 1983.

Linda Smogor took this picture of Harry Hahn, who frequently portrays Lincoln at different events in the Springfield area, as Hahn walked by the Wax Museum.

Fire, When Ready

Yes, it is a house on fire.

And yes, it is a group of firemen posing for pictures and seeming to ignore the heat.

But it's only a fire department "Burn Down" training exercise in Carol Stream, Ill., and it's an abandoned farmhouse the firefighters set themselves for practice.

George Thompson took the picture for the Suburban Tribune, Glendale, in November 1980.

War Games

There's something of the child that remains with all of us—even if we get to be U.S. Army colonels.

This colonel dropped to his knees at a 1982 Veteran's Day ceremony in Norfolk, Va., to play with a miniature cannon.

John Sheally of The Virginian-Pilot/Ledger-Star caught the full bird.

High-Wire Fall

"Our life is show business," Karl Wallenda once said.

"Without show business, we don't survive, and we have to exist."

The 73-year-old patriarch of the most famous high-wire troupe in the world, "The Great Wallendas," had proven his courage and dedication often, thrilling circus audiences for more than half a century.

He had seen his son-in-law and nephew killed, and his adopted son paralyzed, in 1962 when the "human pyramid" he had created toppled in a performance in Detroit. He had seen another son-in-law die 10 years later in another performance in West Virginia.

"We can't lose our nerve," he said. And he went back to show business.

On March 22, 1978, he started to walk along a wire strung 100 feet above the ground between two buildings of the Condado Holiday Inn in San Juan, Puerto Rico. It was to promote the Pan American Circus there, in which he and his 17-year-old granddaughter performed nightly on a 50-foot wire.

About midway across, the wire seemed to be dancing around underneath him. Winds were 12 miles an hour, with stronger gusts.

Wallenda lost his balance, grasped for the wire, then fell 10 stories to the ground, his balancing stick at his feet. He died at a nearby hospital, of multiple fractures.

The photos were taken by Gary Williams of El Nueva Dia©.

Questioning, Rhodesian-Style

For years, black nationalist guerrillas fought to oust the white-dominated Rhodesian government. In five years up to 1977, when this picture was taken, at least 3,668 black guerrillas and 414 Rhodesian soldiers died.

In a rare occurrence, J. Ross Baughman, a contract photographer for The Associated Press, got official approval to accompany Rhodesian troops in action. He came back with reports of army looting, beatings and torture. Government authorities had ordered Baughman back to Salisbury and confiscated or spoiled some of his film, but he was able to get some out.

His photographs won a Pulitzer Prize.

This one was taken in September 1977 near the village of Kikidoo as Baughman accompanied a cavalry unit close to the Botswana border. The soldiers had rounded up a group of local blacks for questioning.

The Rhodesian trooper pictured here held a gun in front of the prisoners, who were forced to hold this position in the heat of the midday sun. The soldier repeatedly clicked his pistol in their faces.

Summary
Execution

The four million Kurds in Iran, with eight million brethren in Iraq and Turkey, have long dreamed of an independent state. In Iran, Kurdish leaders had hoped for autonomy after the revolution of the Ayatollah Ruhollah Khomeini toppled the regime of Shah Mohammed Reza Pahlavi.

But, open fighting broke out between the Kurds and the new rulers, and the Kurds, nomadic Moslems, once again rose to seek independence. In August 1979, in a summary trial presided over by an Islamic judge, 11 rebels were sentenced to death and executed in the Kurdish city of Sanandaj in Iran. Fifty-one Kurds were put to death in a similar manner in two weeks.

Terrorism

"Eliminating terrorism is an absolute impossibility. We're ready for the hijackings and the hostage-taking. But for most of it, we can only sit and wait."

Officials bluntly stated their frustration as terrorist acts continued despite the consequences.

Italy shattered the Red Brigades and West Germany all but eliminated the Baader-Meinhof group and Dutch marines were able to recapture a train hijacked by terrorists.

Yet . . .

Government intelligence agencies listed more than 100 groups that used terror for political goals in 15 years since 1968, from romantics who bombed empty buildings for lost causes to technology-equipped commandoes who killed en masse.

The most shattering, perhaps, took place on the world stage of the Olympics in Munich, Germany, in 1972. The hooded terrorist pictured here was one of the Arab Black September group that invaded the building housing Israeli athletes on that Sept. 5. Before the ordeal was over, 11 Israelis, a German policeman and five terrorists were dead.

Some other sensational terrorist acts pictured here:

—Guerrillas blew up two hijacked airliners at a desert airstrip at Al Khana, Jordan, in September 1970.

—Gunmen invaded the Iranian embassy in London in May 1980. A BBC employee, Sim Harris, one of 15 hostages, scrambled to safety as flames shot from an embassy window. Britain's Special Air Service saved 14 others and captured a number of the gunmen.

—A Lufthansa jetliner was hijacked and brought down at Dubai, United Arab Emirates, Oct. 17, 1977. The photo shows one of the hijackers threatening pilot Jurgen Schumann, who later was killed by the terrorists.

On the Edge

"One of you is going to get killed."

Forty-eight-year-old Oswald Mayes shouted the warning to police officers who had come to try to talk him off a 12-foot entryway roof at his home in Somerset, Mass.

Mayes, yelling and screaming, held a seven-inch kitchen knife in his hand as he kept police at bay for an hour and a half while they tried talk and then force—Mace, riot clubs—in vain. One policeman was cut on the shoulder.

Then Mayes jumped from the roof and was subdued by police. He fractured his leg and broke an ankle.

Norman Sylvia took the pictures for the Providence Journal-Bulletin©.

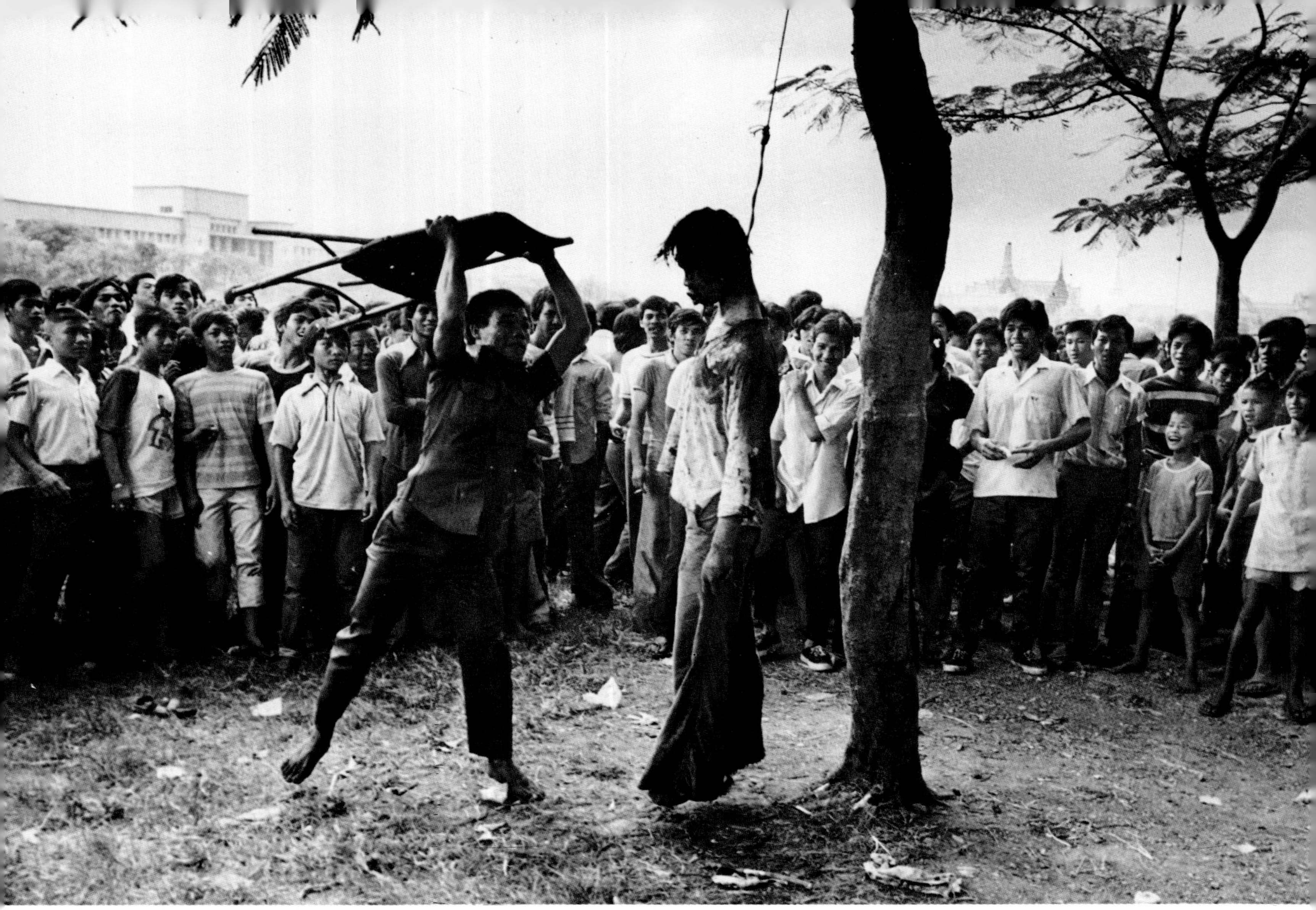

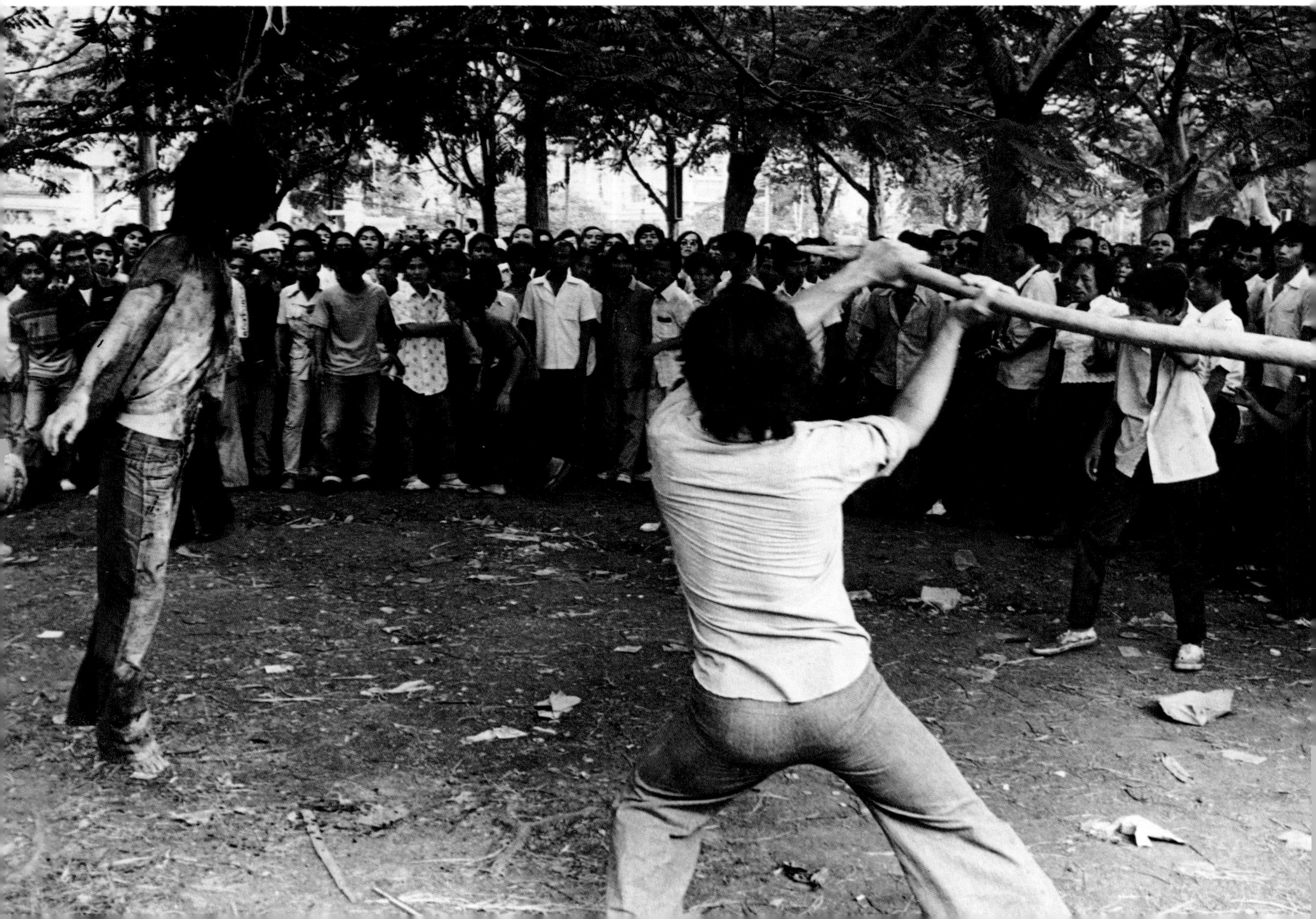

Bloody, Brutal Rioting

Bloody fighting between protestors and police in Bangkok, Thailand, in October 1976 came after nearly 2,000 left-wing students barricaded themselves behind the walls of Thammasat University demanding the expulsion of former military ruler Thanom Kittikachorn. Thanom, ousted in 1973, had returned from exile the previous month.

On the morning of Oct. 6, police stormed the university, firing machineguns, grenades and anti-tank weapons. They used a dump truck to smash through the gates.

The savage fighting left at least 41 dead, nearly 200 wounded and more than 300 students arrested.

Two of the victims were hanged and their bodies mutilated. Others were set afire.

Associated Press photographer-writer Neal Ulevich witnessed the raid and took these dramatic photographs of the violent clash. The pictures earned him a Pulitzer Prize.

He recalled the event:

"Troops armed with M16 rifles were spraying wild fire across a quadrangle, shattering classroom windows and nicking holes in the walls. It was sunny, very hot, and noisy... .

"Some of the troops tossed hand grenades through the windows. The 'garrumph' of a grenade going off was followed by a puff of smoke, and the tinkle of showering glass. Then the recoilless rifle crew moved up.

". . . About 9:30 a.m., the battle seemed over. (But) the shooting began again . . . That happened two more times before I reached the nearest classroom building.

"At the door students were running out, diving to their hands and knees and crawling past soldiers who told them to take off their shirts, and coeds their blouses. Slow performance earned a kick.

"Blood gushed from bullet wounds. A grenade went off in a classroom above us, showering troops and their captives with glass and plaster. The students crawled toward the center of the quadrangle to lie in the hot sun. . . .

"Then we were out on the street—close by the pleasant green trees that surround the Pramaine Ground, site of Bangkok's colorful weekend fair. But then we saw the angry swarm of Thais around two of those trees and their anger was white hot. I saw the limp body of a dead student hanging from one tree. The scene was being repeated just a few feet away.

"I don't know how much earlier the students had been lynched—probably just a few minutes—but enraged rightists felt robbed by death and continued to batter the bodies.

"One rightist hit a hanging corpse with a folding chair until the rope broke and the body tumbled doll-like to the ground. At the other tree a rightist was slashing at the throat of the other lynching victim. But the corpse didn't bleed and that apparently enraged the rightist, who stabbed the neck and face repeatedly.

"A Thai woman who witnessed the spectacle—as did thousands—said she was 'sick with disgust . . . They (the victims) looked like I did. They were butchering people.'

". . . I had seen enough, and left."

Hostage Drama

For three-and-a-half hours on April 25, 1979, Newman Augustine Osebor, a Nigerian exchange student, held psychiatrist Dr. Richard E. Townsend a hostage in his car, on Interstate 8 around San Diego. Townsend was kidnapped and held at gunpoint after being forced to withdraw money from a bank.

Photos by AP staffer Leonard Ignelzi show Osebor as he shouted to police and leaped out of the car, firing his gun. Police returned the fire and killed him.

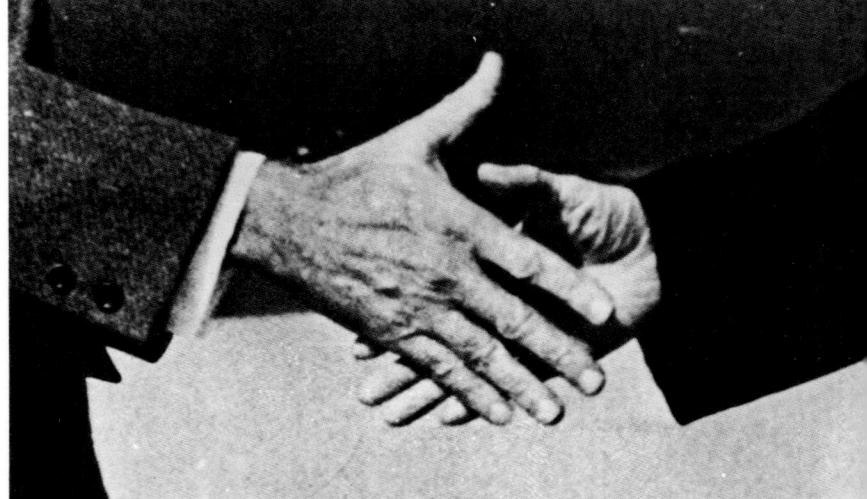

Historic Meeting

The handshakes reached across decades of hostility.

Since 1949, with the success of the Communist revolution in China, that vast Asian nation had closed its doors to the West. Similarly, United States policy had been to quarantine and isolate the Chinese People's Republic.

Indeed, the early career of Richard M. Nixon, who assumed the U.S. presidency in 1969, had been marked by implacable anti-Communist crusading.

It was all the more astonishing, then, when Nixon announced he would bridge the gap and make an official visit to China in February 1972.

The moment of the historic meeting is symbolized by the blowup of the handshake between President Nixon and Chinese Premier Chou En-lai at Peking Airport on Feb. 21, the seventh day of the Year of the Rat in the Oriental calendar. After Nixon and Chou reviewed the honor guard at the airport, the American president was whisked off to the private study of Chairman Mao Tse-tung for an informal and secret meeting.

Nixon spent a week in China discussing international relations and getting in some touring as well. He joined Chinese leaders at the Great Wall and visited Hangchow and Shanghai.

The trip proved to be the high point of Nixon's administration and had as-yet untold effects on global relations.

Nixon called it "the week that changed the world." In a final toast, he said to Chou: "Mr. Prime Minister, our two people tonight hold the future of the world in our hands."

Chou's remarks had been similar: "The gates to friendship have been opened."

118

Farewell Address

After more than a year of national agony, headlines of Watergate, "third rate burglary" and presidential scandal, court maneuvers, talk of impeachment, convictions, imprisonments . . . the president of the United States made his decision. Richard M. Nixon became the first U.S. head of state to resign while in office.

Before announcing the inevitable to the nation, Nixon gathered his White House staff in the East Room to say goodbye on Aug. 9, 1974. Associated Press photographer Chick Harrity was there to record the historic farewell and the empathetic emotions of Pat Nixon and daughter Tricia.

Then Nixon boarded a helicopter for a flight to nearby Andrews Air Force Base—and into history.

Death Fall

Feb. 22, 1971. Sydney, Australia, airport.

The Japan Air Lines DC-8 was on its way to Tokyo. Somehow, 14-year-old Keith Emanuel Sapsford had stowed away by climbing up into the wheel housing, unseen. At 200 feet, the pilot retracted the wheels. The youth fell to his death.

Amateur photographer John Gilpin was at the airport trying out a new lens when he took this shot — not knowing what had happened until the film was developed.

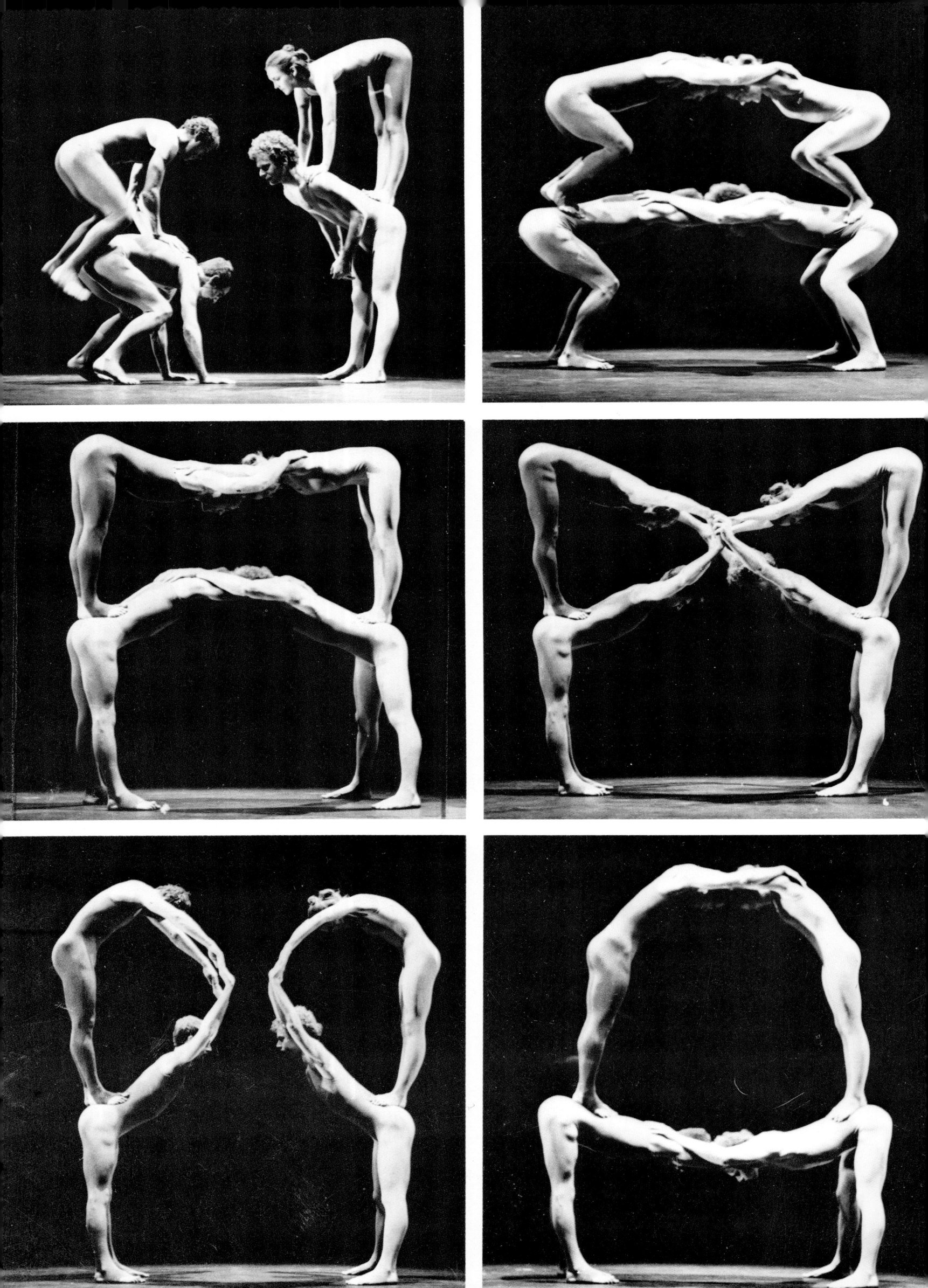

Dance Design

The four men and two women of the Pilobolus Dance Theater troupe balance on each other's backs, necks and hips in group designs that have become their signature.

The unusual routine was caught in the lens of the camera held by AP's Suzanne Vlamis when the dancers performed "Ocellus" in New York in 1977.

Victory and Defeat

Who won?

It's not difficult to determine the first across the line in this bicycle race.

Photographer Scott Linnett of the Vista (Calif.) Press snapped the reactions as the cyclist on the right caught the leader at the finish line and won by a spoke.

Home Run Hero

It was Hank Aaron's second time at bat in the game against the Los Angeles Dodgers. His first time up in front of 53,775 hometown fans in Atlanta that night, the slugger had walked on five pitches.

Now, in the fourth inning, on a 1-0 fastball thrown by Al Downing, Aaron belted a 400-foot shot that sailed out of Atlanta Stadium.

With that 715th career home run on April 8, 1974, Henry Aaron became baseball's all-time home run king. It came in the third game of his 21st season and just four days after he had tied the legendary Babe Ruth's mark of 714 with a home run in Cincinnati off Jack Billingham.

Aaron added 40 more round-trippers to his record total before retiring at the end of the 1976 season.

The photograph, by AP's Harry Harris, also shows Dodger catcher Joe Ferguson and umpire David Davidson watching the historic moment.

Say "Chee-tah"

Maybe the photographer was taking a little too long and these cubs, like all children, got a bit edgy.

Or maybe they are trying to say "cheese."

The four cheetah cubs were just two weeks old when they got together to pose for this picture at the Cincinnati Zoo before being put on public display.

Photo by Fred Straub, Cincinnati Enquirer.

Naked Came the Stranger

Streaking . . . an unfashionable fad of the '70s.

Some considered it asinine.

Obviously, it depended on the point of view.

Actor David Niven got a chuckle when a streaker, waving two fingers in a peace symbol, ran across the stage at the 1974 Academy Awards, giving national television viewers a brief glimpse.

What do you say to a naked gentleman?

"Isn't it a laugh," said Niven, "that the only laugh that man will get in his life will be by stripping off his clothes and showing his shortcomings."

Drag Race Mishap

Cameraman Joe Rooks, of Bowling Green, Ohio, was filming the National Hot Rod Association Nationals in Indianapolis on Sept. 1, 1979, when a dragster turned over several times and smashed into the rail, sending parts flying into the field.

AP photographer Chuck Robinson caught the tragic action as the supercharger off the engine bounced up and hit the cameraman in the back. Rooks died on the way to the hospital.

The driver, Frank Rupert, of Corritos, Calif., suffered a broken leg and internal injuries.

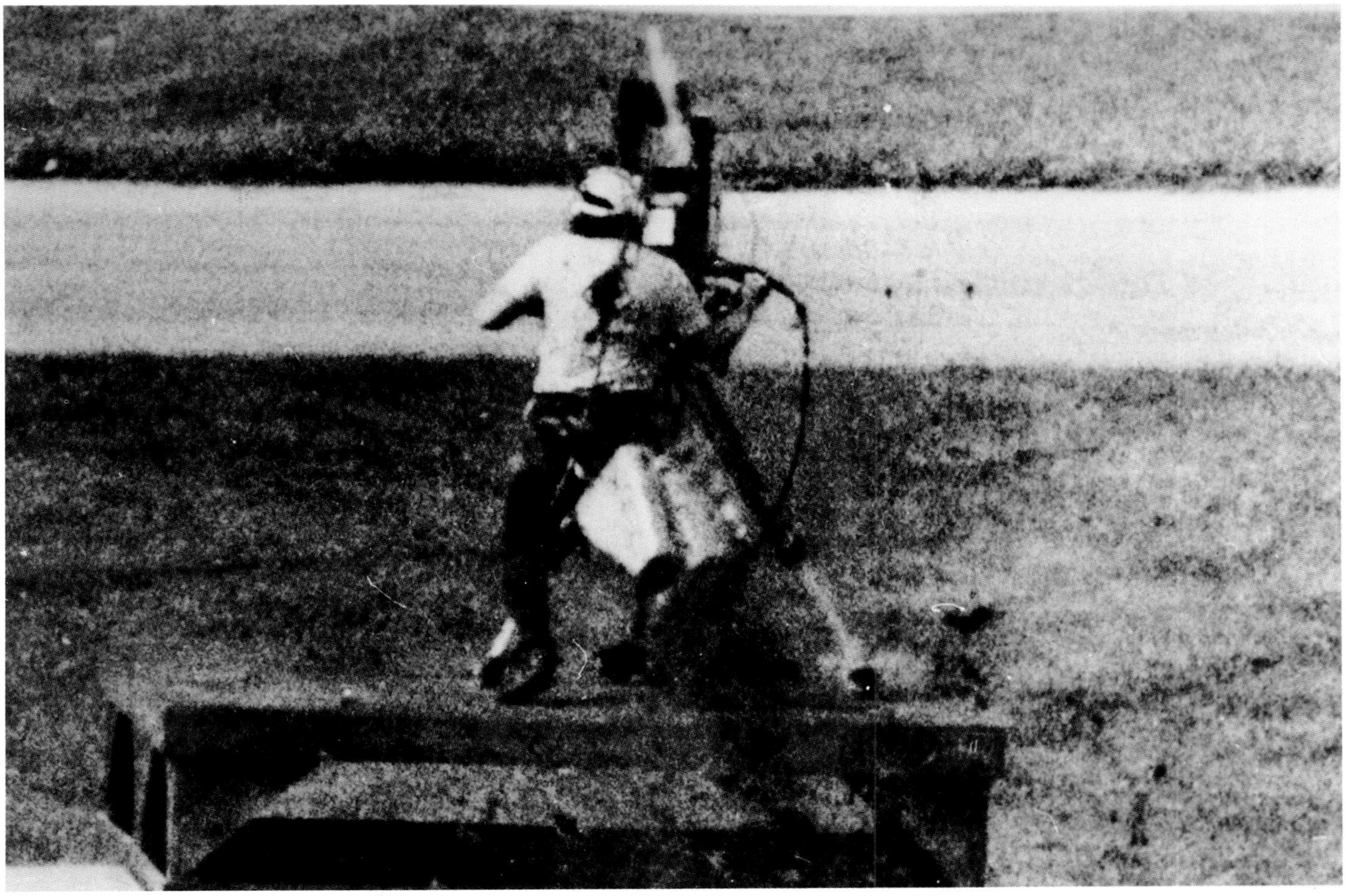

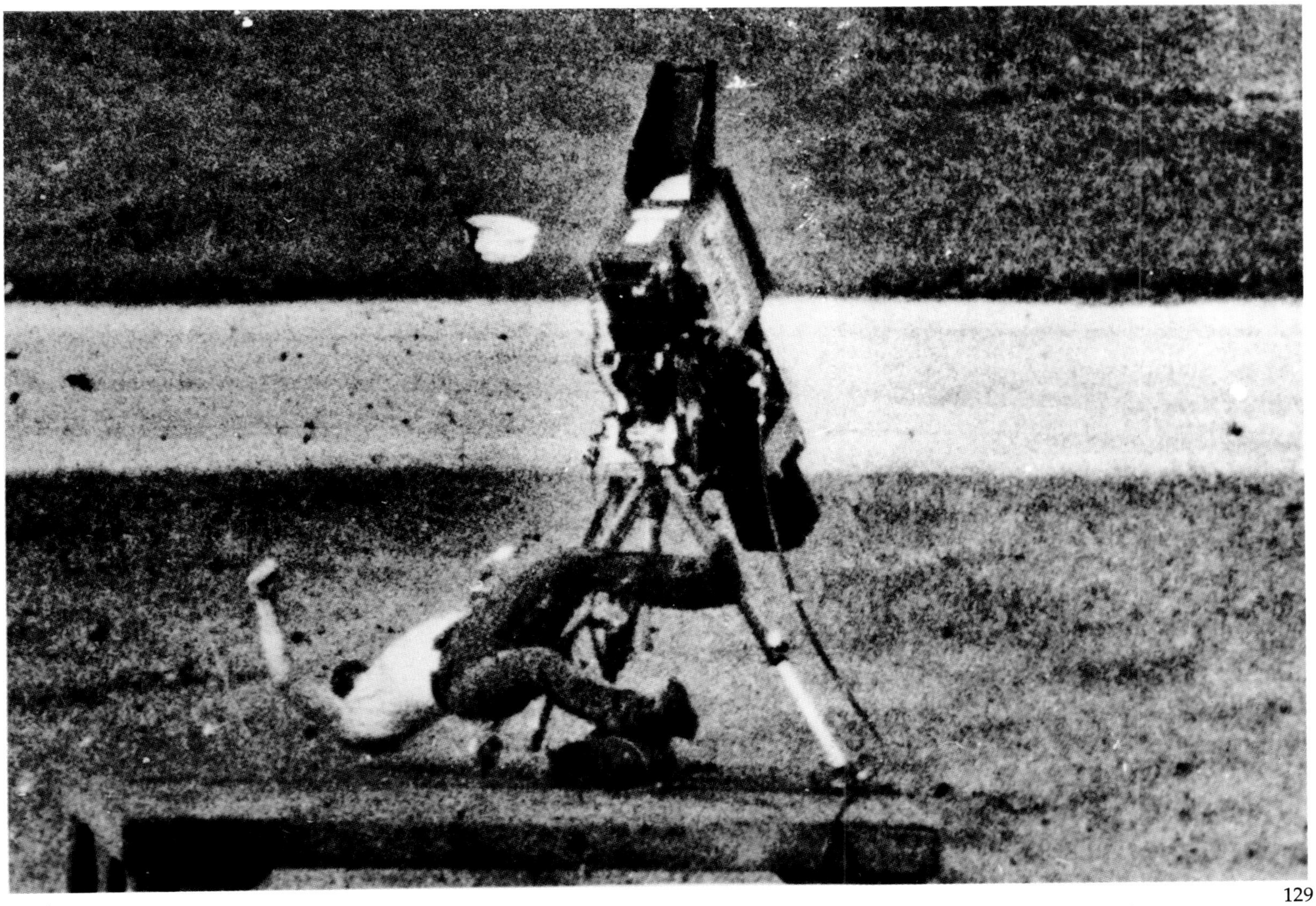

Nature on a Rampage

First comes the cloud. An ominous-looking cloud.
It's nature threatening. Tornado coming.
Henry Perez, a Kansas highway patrol trooper, saw it coming one stormy night in May 1970. He was about 25 miles west of Salina — with a camera.
The result is a photographic record of the formation of a tornado.

Meteorologists tell us that tornadoes are violent thunderstorms, with winds whirling inwards and creating a center of low pressure. As the winds increase, a partial vacuum is generated at the center. Condensation occurs around the funnel-shaped whirl—the ominous cloud, as it picks up dust and debris.

Tornadoes could contain winds up to 500 mph when the whirl touches the ground, ripping up all in its path.

Fortunately, this one, in open country, caused only minor damage.

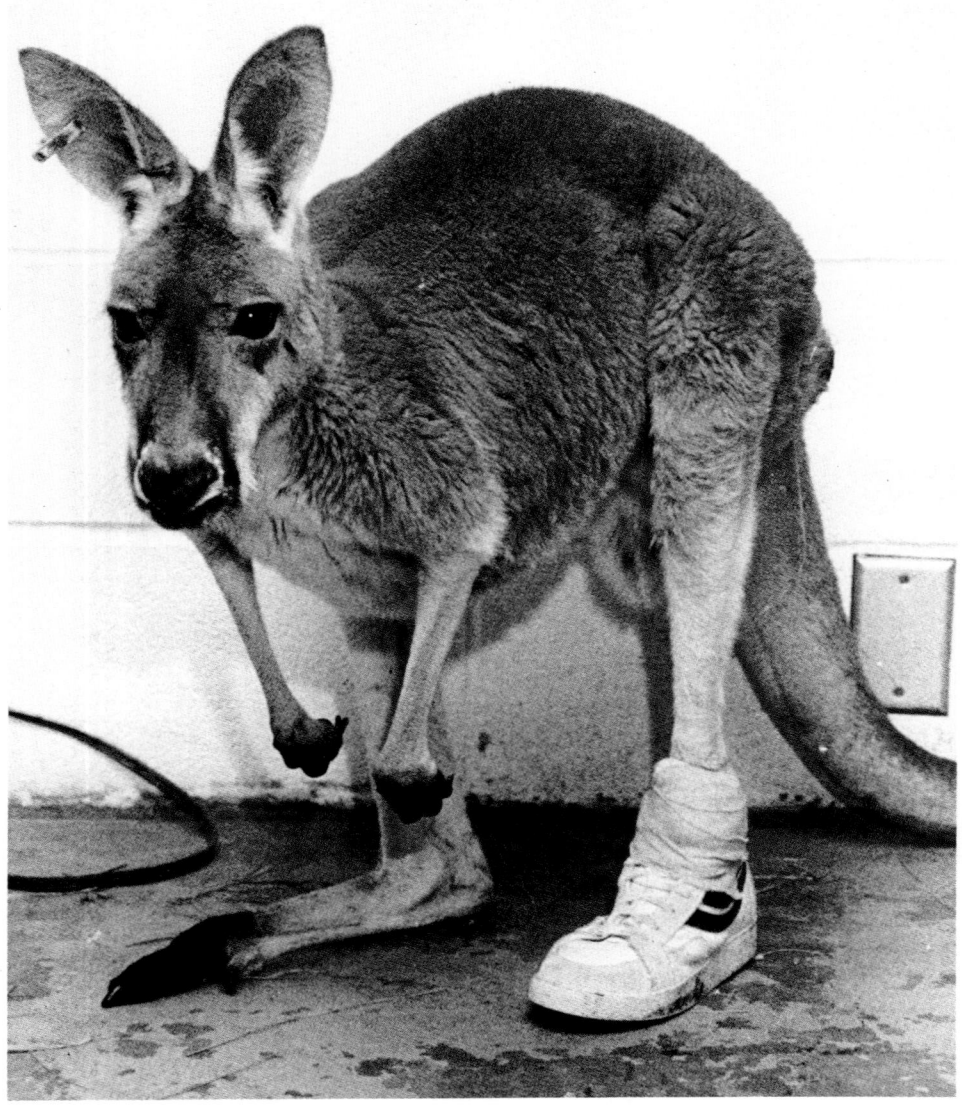

Rueful and Wooful 'Roos

Maybe he didn't look before he leaped.

Staff veterinarians at the Kansas City Zoo put the sneaker—children's size 13—on the young kangaroo after part of his foot was amputated because of a severe infection. Kansas City photographer Pete Leabo reported that the kangaroo had no trouble hopping around in his new footwear.

The other kangaroo pair were in an affectionate embrace when caught by photographer Hans Rauchensteiner, Agency Sven Simon, of Munich, West Germany. It earned him a World Press first prize in the "Happy News" category in 1978.

Opera, Barely

Opera star Carol Neblett took her role as a courtesan seriously and appeared nude at the end of the second act of a performance of "Thais" at the New Orleans Theatre of Performing Arts in 1973.

Clenched Fist Defiance

The defiance was clear in the determined faces, in the symbolism of the raised clenched fists.

Inmates at the maximum security prison at Attica, N.Y., had complained of conditions and contended that many of them were political prisoners.

The day before this picture was taken by Bob Schutz on Sept. 10, 1971, more than 1,000 prisoners had taken 43 guards and prison workers hostage and held them in D yard, making their demands. Commissioner of Correction Russell Oswald had negotiated and eventually agreed to some demands — but not amnesty.

The scuffle that had grown into a full-scale confrontation and riot then turned into a bloody one-day encounter. On Sept. 13, helicopters dropped tear gas into the prison yard. State troopers and guards assaulted.

In six minutes, 29 prisoners and 10 hostages were killed. Eighty-nine others were wounded.

Courtroom Tragedy

James David McClain, a prisoner from nearby San Quentin, was up before Judge Harold J. Haley in Marin County (Calif.) Civic Center court on Aug. 7, 1970, charged with knifing a prison guard.

Suddenly, Jonathan Jackson, a youth who came in as a spectator, stood up and shouted, "This is it. I've got an automatic weapon. Everybody freeze."

He had concealed the weapons in his coat.

McClain taped a sawed-off shotgun to his wrist and around Judge Haley's neck so it would go off if he tried to pull free. They took three women jurors and the district attorney as hostages and demanded the release of the Soledad Brothers, convicts in Soledad Prison charged with murdering a guard. One of them was Jackson's brother.

Outside, as the gunmen got into a yellow van with the hostages, there was a shootout with police.

Judge Haley, Jackson and William Christmas, a convict witness, were killed.

Photographers Jim Keane and Roger Borkrath of the San Rafael Independent-Journal had responded to the police radio call: armed man in the courtroom.

"Take lots of pictures," one of the gunmen had said, "we are the revolutionaries."

City Lights

For visitor and native alike, New York City at night is a stirring sight indeed. The view from Brooklyn, under the Brooklyn Bridge, is the lower Manhattan skyline.

Then, on July 14, 1977, the lights went out.

The famous skyline was dark after a power failure hit the city.

One building at the left appears to be lit with emergency power. A stream of light seen at the edge of the East River came from the headlights of cars on the FDR Drive. Photo is by Ray Stubblebine.

Dashing Commuter?

Looking much like a commuter rushing to make his train, President Richard Nixon checks his watch, but keeps one hand free to "press the flesh" in Brussels in 1974.

Photographer Charles Tasnadi made the hurry-up shot near the Royal Palace as Nixon worried about his luncheon with King Baudouin.

Mob Execution

No, it's not a scene from "The Godfather." It's horribly real.

Carmine "Lilo" Galante, an organized crime leader, was shot at point-blank range as he dined on the patio of a back yard garden in a Brooklyn, N.Y., restaurant on July 12, 1979.

Indicative of the surprise with which the killers struck, Galante still had his cigar clenched in his teeth when police arrived at the blood-spattered patio.

Two other men—a Galante bodyguard and the owner of the restaurant—also were killed.

Photo by Bob Karp.

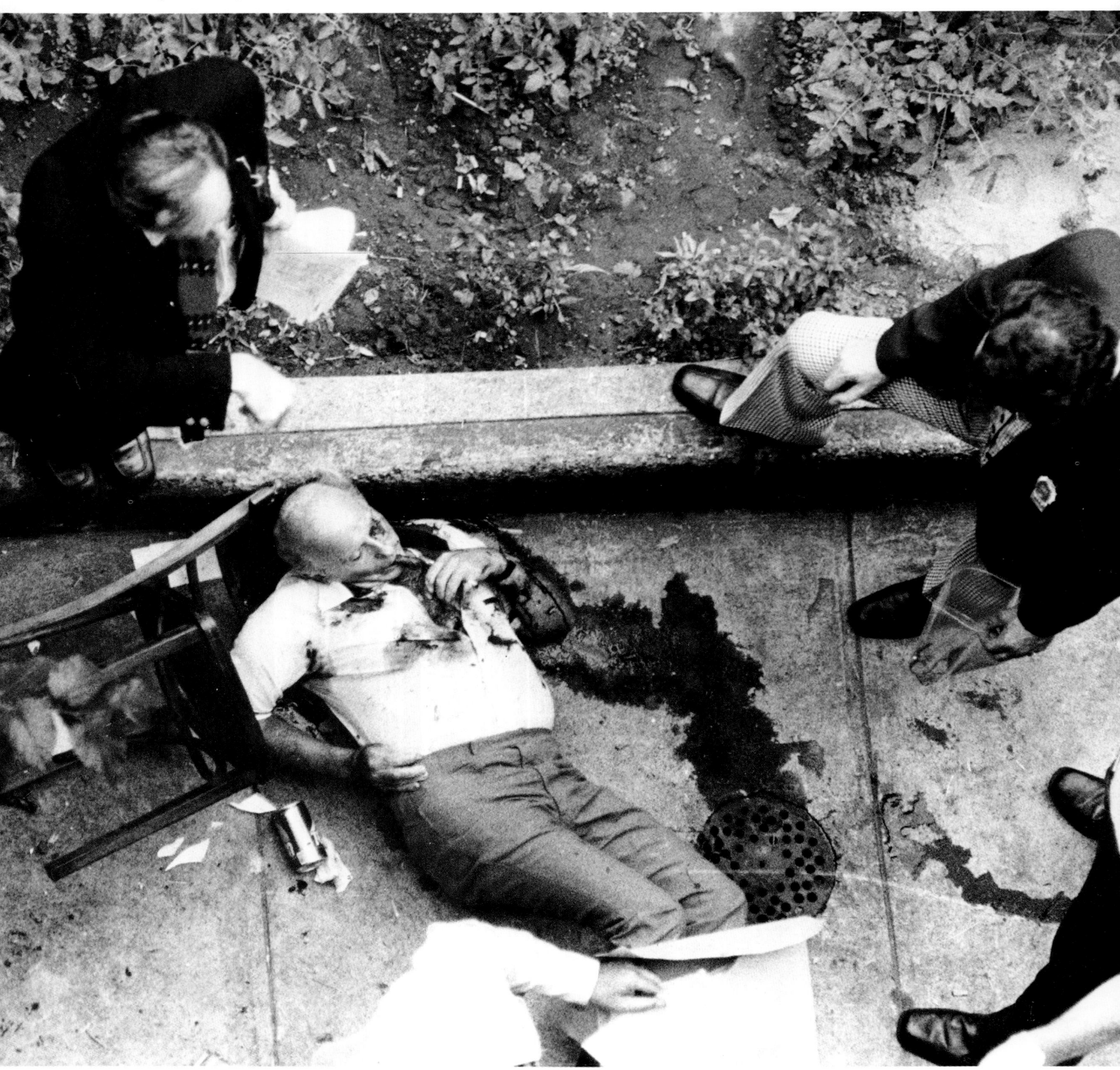

Fatal Hollywood Drama

Photographer Anthony K. Roberts was in the parking lot outside a Hollywood, Calif., discount store when he heard the commotion.

His pictures tell the story. Edward Fisher tried to kidnap Ellen Sheldon, holding a knife to her throat. Fisher had her lying on the ground, but she struggled to her feet.

Seconds later, after repeated warnings, security guard George Derby shot Fisher dead.

Roberts' pictures won a Pulitzer Prize in 1973.

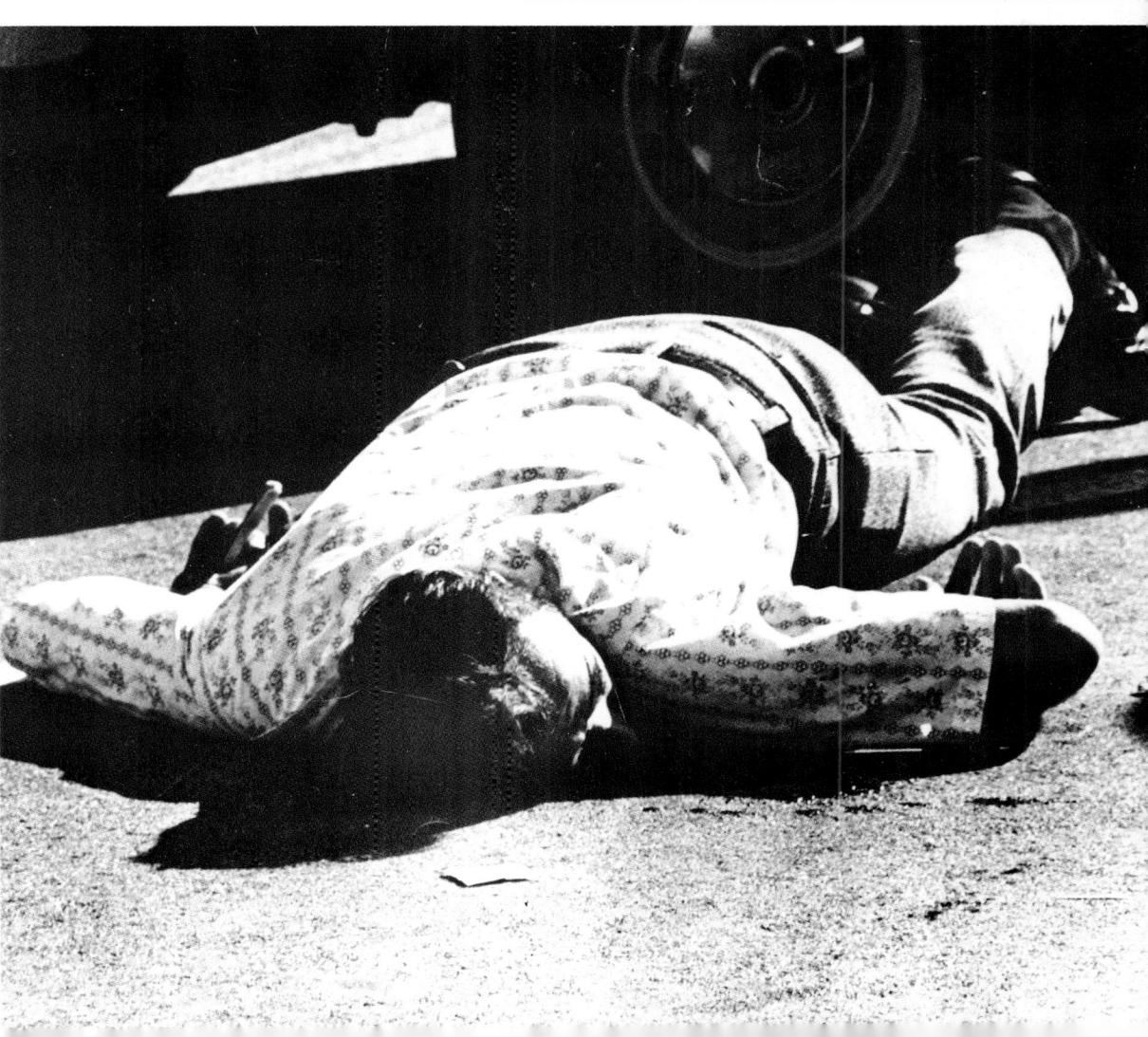

Amish Polio Scare

The Old World Amish community of southeastern Pennsylvania had to face a New World problem—polio—in the spring of 1979.

Because of a polio scare in the state, the residents of Lancaster County were urged to take the oral polio vaccine. The Amish sect shuns immunization.

Many Amish families faced the dilemma.

Photographer Jim Gerberich of the Lancaster New Era went to one of the free clinics set up for the immunizations and took the picture of this Amish family. Gerberich found out later that the family did not take the serum because the father had cancer and one of the children had suffered from polio earlier in life. Several months after the picture was taken, the father died of cancer.

During that vaccination weekend in June 1979, 148,000 Lancaster County residents showed up at the polio vaccine clinics.

"But," recalled Gerberich, "of all the faces I photographed, the five in this family stay in my mind."

Welcome Home, Daddy

The Vietnam War, that seemingly endless quicksand of conflict, came to an official close for the United States in January 1973 with the signing of a peace agreement.

With America's longest war over, its 562 prisoners of war would come home. Some had endured as much as eight-and-a-half years of imprisonment under sometimes brutal conditions.

In February, the first POWs came back.

The nation rejoiced, but the joy of the families was the more telling.

On March 17, 1973, Lt. Col. Robert L. Stirm, of Foster City, Calif., landed at Travis Air Force Base to a greeting no tickertape parade could match, no marching bands or medals could surpass.

Rushing to greet him first is his daughter, Lori. Not far behind are sons Robert and Roger, daughter Cynthia, and wife Loretta.

Somewhere behind Stirm is Associated Press photographer Sal Veder, capturing the moment for a Pulitzer Prize.

Signs of the Time

More than 10,000 marchers made sure everyone within sight, including cameraman Dave Tenenbaum, knew that ERA stood for Equal Rights Amendment.

The men and women came from some 30 different states to march toward the Capitol in Springfield, Ill., in May 1976 in an effort to persuade the Illinois Legislature to ratify the amendment. Nonetheless, their effort failed.

Forelegs vs. Two

It looked like a photo finish with the jockey ahead by a foot.

Actually, both were losers.

The official race track photo was taken at Cincinnati's River Downs on Aug. 6, 1977, when jockey R.O. Bentley fell off his mount Luna Bonita at the finish line after the horse got flustered, ducked its head and unseated him. Both were disqualified.

RIVER DOWNS RACE AUG 6 1977

Feelings

Fishing may or may not be man's favorite sport, but for this young blind boy it meant a whole new world of sensation.

Michael Goren was 4 years old when he attended the Upsal School for the Blind in Media, Pa., and went fishing from the bank of its stocked private pond. Photographer Dom Ligato snapped the moment when the youngster touched the first fish he had ever caught. Needless to say, he wasn't about to let it go.

Towering Inferno

Fire destroyed the 20-story Grande Avenida office building in downtown Sao Paulo, Brazil, on Feb. 14, 1981, killing 18 people and injuring 44 others. This man and his two children. trapped by the flames, were rescued by the helmeted fireman.

Photo by Folma de Sao Paulo.

Violence in Boston

Busing, the idea of transporting children to a school in an integration effort, created a great deal of controversy in many places in which it was attempted.

In Boston, Mass., in April 1976, the controversy exploded into violence.

Photographer Stan Forman of the Boston Herald-American© caught the moment when emotions reached that point of physical conflict. Anti-busing demonstrators held Ted Landsmark, executive director of the Boston Contractors Association, while others emphasized their point with the American flag.

Landsmark was attacked on his way to a City Hall meeting by students and their parents who were boycotting school.

"…Two More Seconds…Two More…"

As photographer Stanley Forman of the Boston Herald-American raced to cover a fire in the city's Back Bay section that July 22, 1975, he heard the fire dispatcher saying something about people trapped.

Looking up as he ran, he could see a firefighter lowering himself from the roof to a fire escape where a young woman and a child were clinging.

"I knew," Forman recalled, "that in seconds they would all be on the fire escape."

He climbed on to the bed of the ladder truck, about 10 feet above the ground. He was shooting pictures when he saw the fireman's hand go up to grab an aerial ladder being positioned for the rescue.

"Suddenly someone screamed; or maybe it was the shriek of the metal as the fire escape gave way . . .

"I remember thinking, 'I don't want to see them hit the

ground.' I turned away before it happened. I must have stood with my back to what was happening there on the ground for close to a minute. People were screaming. I was shaking. I didn't want to look."

Fireman Robert O'Neill was able to hold on to the ladder and lift himself up.

Nineteen-year-old Diana Bryant was not as fortunate. She fell to her death as the fire escape collapsed. Her goddaughter, 2-year-old Tiare Jones, survived the five-story plunge.

"Two more seconds, two more seconds . . ." O'Neill kept repeating as he reached the ground.

The spectacular photos earned Forman a Pulitzer Prize and created a stir of reader and editor reaction.

Some thought the photos should not have been

published, and criticized newspapers that used the pictures for ''cheap journalism,'' poor taste, or invasion of privacy. One reader wrote: ''You're giving our kids a nightmare.''

Harold Buell, executive newsphoto editor of The Associated Press, said: ''You're cursed if you do, and cursed for manipulating the news if you don't.''

Nora Ephron, in her media column in Esquire, wrote: ''They deserve to be printed because they are great pictures, breathtaking pictures of something that happened. That they disturb readers is exactly as it should be: that's why photojournalism is often more powerful than written journalism.''

There was another side to the effects of the photographs on the public. Fire reforms were instigated in the Boston area soon after the photos were published.

Purolator Security, Inc.

Sniper in San Antonio

It was to be a day of fun and frolic—a fiesta parade.

But that April 28, 1979, turned to tragedy as a sniper fired into the crowd awaiting the start of the parade.

Spectators scampered to safety; a woman, blood streaming down her face, crouched low with a young girl; firemen, police and others rushed children away from the scene.

The sniper was killed.

Torture...Then Execution

The result of the Bengali nationalist movement in 1971 was the creation of the independent state of Bangladesh—"Bengal Nation"—in what had been previously called East Pakistan.

Independence followed months of rioting and civil war that ended only with the defeat of the West Pakistani army by Indian troops.

Now, at a race track outside the city of Dacca, the Mukti Bahini, Bengali guerrillas, sought revenge. Before a crowd of some 5,000 men and children, they tortured and executed four non-Bengali East Pakistanis suspected of collaborating with the enemy.

AP photographers Horst Faas and Michel Laurent were there that Dec. 18. They saw the Mukti Bahini burning their captives with lighted cigarettes and beating them. Faas and Laurent walked away, believing that the torture was for the benefit of the cameras. But it went on.

The two photographers returned and took these pictures of the torture and bayoneting.

"During the terrible torture," Faas recalled, "sweat ran down my face and my hands were trembling so much I couldn't change the film. . . . The crowd cheered and took no notice of us.

"Then the mob came in to finish the execution with their trampling feet.

"Someone challenged us for taking those pictures but I think it was our job to report all that happened."

Indian authorities withheld five of their pictures, including two of those reproduced here. Faas was able to get the censored photos out later on a plane to London.

The sensational yet significant photos earned a Pulitzer Prize for Faas (his second) and Laurent.

'Twas Willig and the Slithy...

New Yorkers are considered pretty blasé about even the most bizarre occurrences, but this one got their attention all right.

George Willig, a slight, bearded toymaker and amateur climber, accepted the World Trade Center as "a personal challenge, a challenge to my ingenuity. I just wanted the prize of getting to the top."

Getting to the top meant 110 stories of the South Tower—1,350 feet up a sheer wall. Using equipment he designed and built himself—and tested at night—he accomplished his climb in three-and-a-half hours early that morning of May 26, 1977.

New York police rode up the side of the building on a window washing platform in an effort to talk him out of it, but Willig politely refused.

When he reached the top, he was given summonses for criminal trespass, reckless endangerment and disorderly conduct and threatened with a $250,000 suit.

The city later settled the suit for $1.10—a penny a floor.

Photos by Dave Pickoff.

Mass Murder-Suicide

"To die in revolutionary suicide is to live forever."

What followed that statement from the Rev. Jim Jones, in Jonestown, Guyana, Nov. 18, 1978, still seems incomprehensible: a mass murder-suicide of more than 900 members of the Peoples Temple.

It began after U.S. Rep. Leo Ryan of California, investigating reports of abuse in Jonestown, was shot dead along with three newsmen and a Temple defector in an attack by Temple assassins at an airstrip near the settlement.

Within hours, Jones was urging his flock to kill themselves before they were killed by others.

Some drank freely from vats of fruit drink laced with cyanide. Medical aides squirted the poison into the mouths of squirming children.

Others were beaten and forcibly injected or gunned down. Jones died of a single gunshot wound by an unknown hand.

When the death throes ended, the bodies of 913 people were piled three-deep in the muddy compound.

The picture of mass death was taken by Frank Johnston of the Washington Post, serving as the pool photographer.

Fatal Flight

The Pacific Southwest Airways Boeing 727 was making its final approach to Lindbergh Airport in San Diego, Calif., when it collided with a small plane on a training flight.

Photographer Hans Wendt caught the moment the flaming airliner hurtled toward the ground, where it slammed into a San Diego neighborhood. The final toll that Sept. 25, 1978, was 150 killed, including a dozen on the ground.

Refugees

The world has known of far too many refugees over the centuries. They flee from natural devastation, manmade war, fear and persecution.

The dolefulness of their common plight can be seen not only in their meager possessions and their tattered dress, but deep in their eyes, as Lennox McLendon's photos express.

Young and old alike have suffered the forlorn fate of those forced to flee.

These were among the thousands who sought haven from the havoc of civil war in Nicaragua in 1979, when leftist Sandinistas toppled the government of strongman Anastasio Somoza.

One McLendon photo shows a woman with a white flag walking past a tank in an eastern Managua barrio.

Others show refugees in overcrowded centers in Managua where they came seeking food and shelter.

The three clinging together for emotional comfort are sisters.

Misconducting

Triskaidekaphobia?

Undaunted by the No. 13 on his mount, Ballybutler, jockey J. Darlington is nonetheless unseated while going over a jump at the Kineton Opportunity Handicap Steeplechase at Cheltenham, England, Dec. 5, 1980. The jockey managed, however precariously, to hold on by the stirrups and reins as he and horse parted company. Needless to say, they didn't win.

Orchestra conductor Leonard Bernstein grabbed the attention of author Lilliar.
Hellman in New York in 1977. The two were chatting at a party at which
Miss Hellman was presented with the Dorothy Shaver Rose Award.

Fog...
And Smog

"The fog comes on little cat feet.
"It sits looking over harbor and city on
silent haunches and then moves on."
                    —Carl Sandburg, "The Fog"

In this case in February 1984, the fog sat over midtown Manhattan, leaving only the pointed top of the famous Chrysler Building and the roof of the Pam Am Building visible. AP's Dave Pickoff photographed it from high on the RCA Building.

Another dim view of the city, taken early Thanksgiving morning in 1966 by Neal Boenzi of The New York Times, shows heavy stagnant air pollution conditions caused by a massive air inversion over the Middle Atlantic coast. The smoggy—smoke plus fog—view is south from the Empire State Building.

A Thread of History

June 2, 1953. Queen Elizabeth II stood on the balcony of Buckingham Palace after her coronation, with her somewhat overwhelmed children Prince Charles and Princess Anne between her and the Duke of Edinburgh.

July 29, 1981. Same balcony, same building. The child-to-be-king of 28 years before now stood between his mother, the queen, and his bride, Lady Diana.

444 Days

It was a Sunday, Nov. 4, 1979.

At the U.S. Embassy in Tehran, the usual throngs were gathered on the street outside the compound, shouting their denunciations at those inside and demanding, "Give us the Shah!"

Armed mobs outside the embassy were not new. Indeed, the embassy had been attacked and three people killed in February of that year.

But on this Sunday, in a theatrical burst of Iranian fury over the admission of their deposed Shah Mohammed Reza Pahlavi to the United States for medical treatment, the rioters seized the Americans inside, beginning 444 days of frustration and humiliation for the United States.

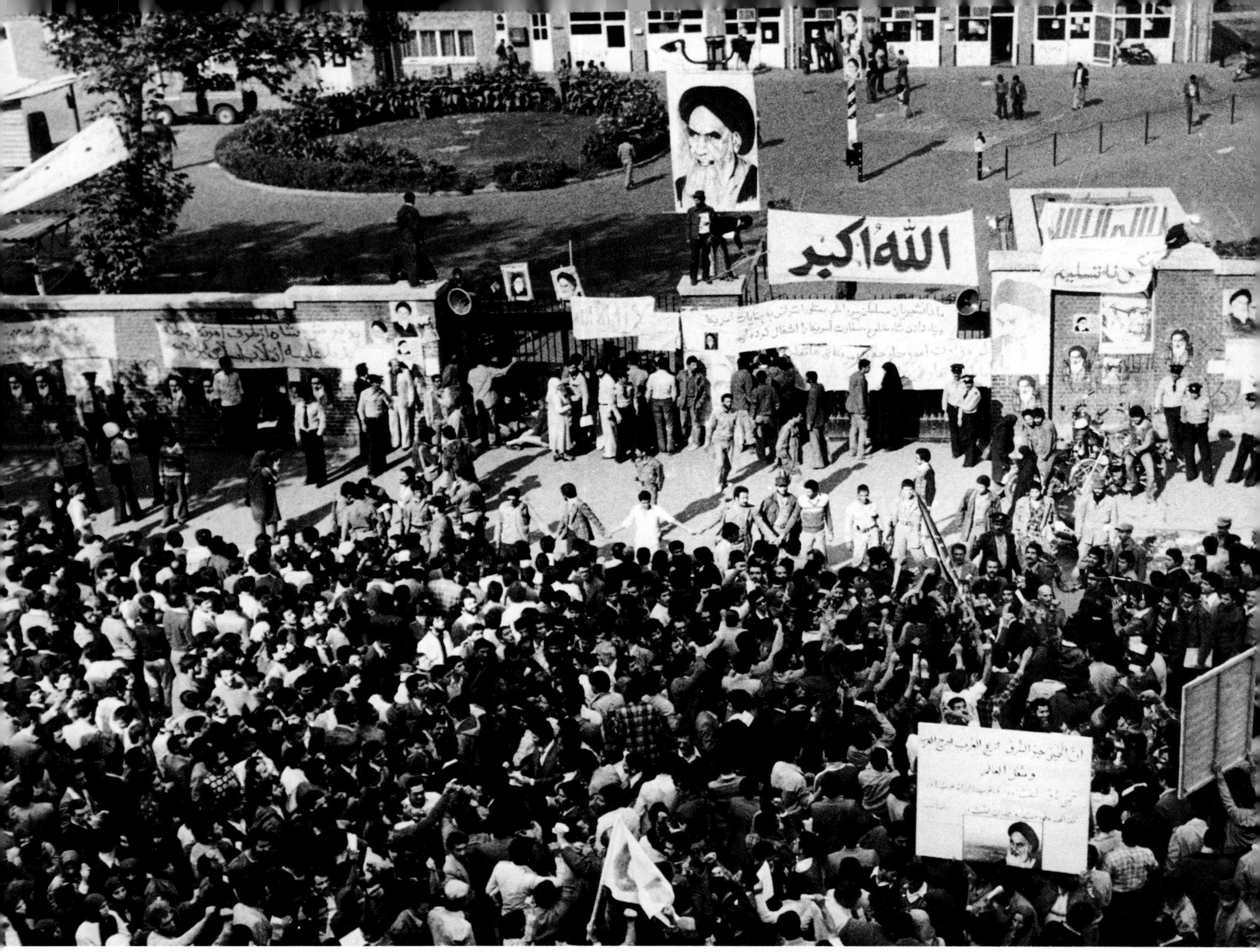
الله اكبر

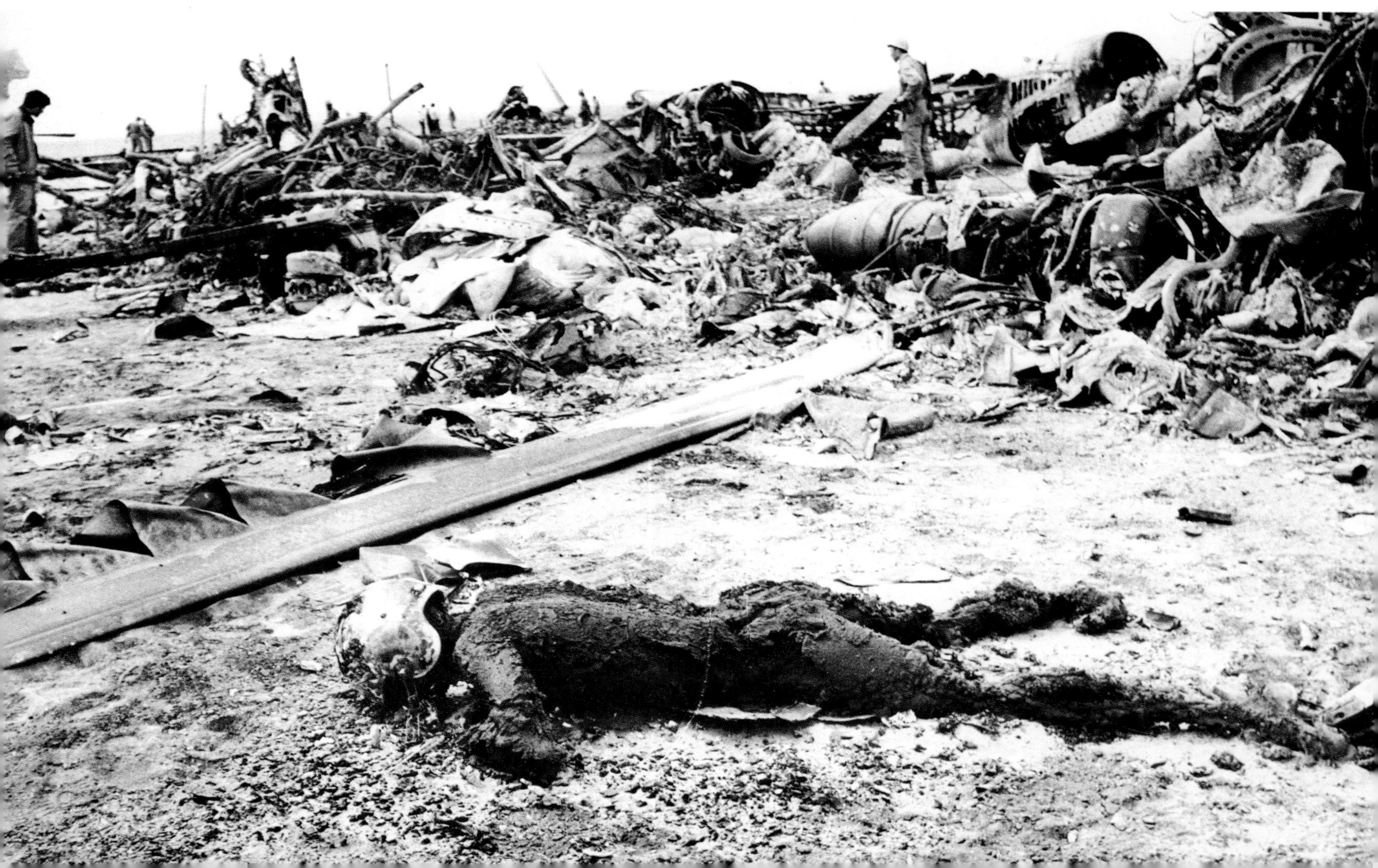

The "student militants" who seized the hostages said they would be held until the Shah and his wealth were returned to the new Islamic Republic of the Ayatollah Ruhollah Khomeini.

The early televised demonstrations at the embassy brought the pain directly into American homes. The world watched as hostages were paraded in front of the embassy; blindfolds became symbols of the humiliation. They watched as the U.S. flag was burned.

American outrage and anger deepened. But little, if anything, could be done without sacrificing the lives of the captives.

Economic sanctions were tried, but they did not have much effect.

Then, on April 24, 1980, after some six months of captivity, a military rescue attempt was made.

It ended, a failure, in the Iranian desert, at Posht-i-Badam, or Desert One, 250 miles southeast of Tehran. "Equipment failure" was among the reasons that the daring rescue attempt was aborted. Two U.S. aircraft collided on the ground. Eight men died in the flames. Five other members of the anti-terrorist strike force known as Operation Blue Light were injured.

Anger and frustration boiled up again.

Meantime, the Shah died in July, in his final refuge of Egypt.

And the hostages spent a second Christmas in Iran.

The end came in the final days of the Jimmy Carter presidency.

A deal was made and the hostages were released Jan. 20, 1981.

The joy and national relief was evident in the reaction of David Roeder, one of the 52 hostages, as he felt the freedom at Rhein Main Air Base in Frankfurt, West Germany, first stop on the way home.

WELCOME BACK TO FREEDOM

OPEN

Untouched by Human Hands

Sometimes, just sometimes, the human eye, with all its visions of beauty, art or truth, is not enough.

Automation must take over, by necessity, for the more personal view through the camera lens.

Two of the best-known "absentee" photographers work in banks and in outer space. Despite their lack of human insight, they have provided some of the most dramatic and stunning photographs of our time.

A rogue's gallery of bank robberies in action is highlighted by the sequence showing Patricia Hearst taking part in the Hibernia holdup in California in 1974.

The newspaper empire heiress had been kidnapped by members of the radical Symbionese Liberation Army, but she had changed loyalties and joined its revolutionary cause. These photos, taken by automatic camera at the bank, played a major role in Miss Hearst's trial in San Francisco in 1977. She was convicted of bank robbery, but later had her sentence commuted by President Carter.

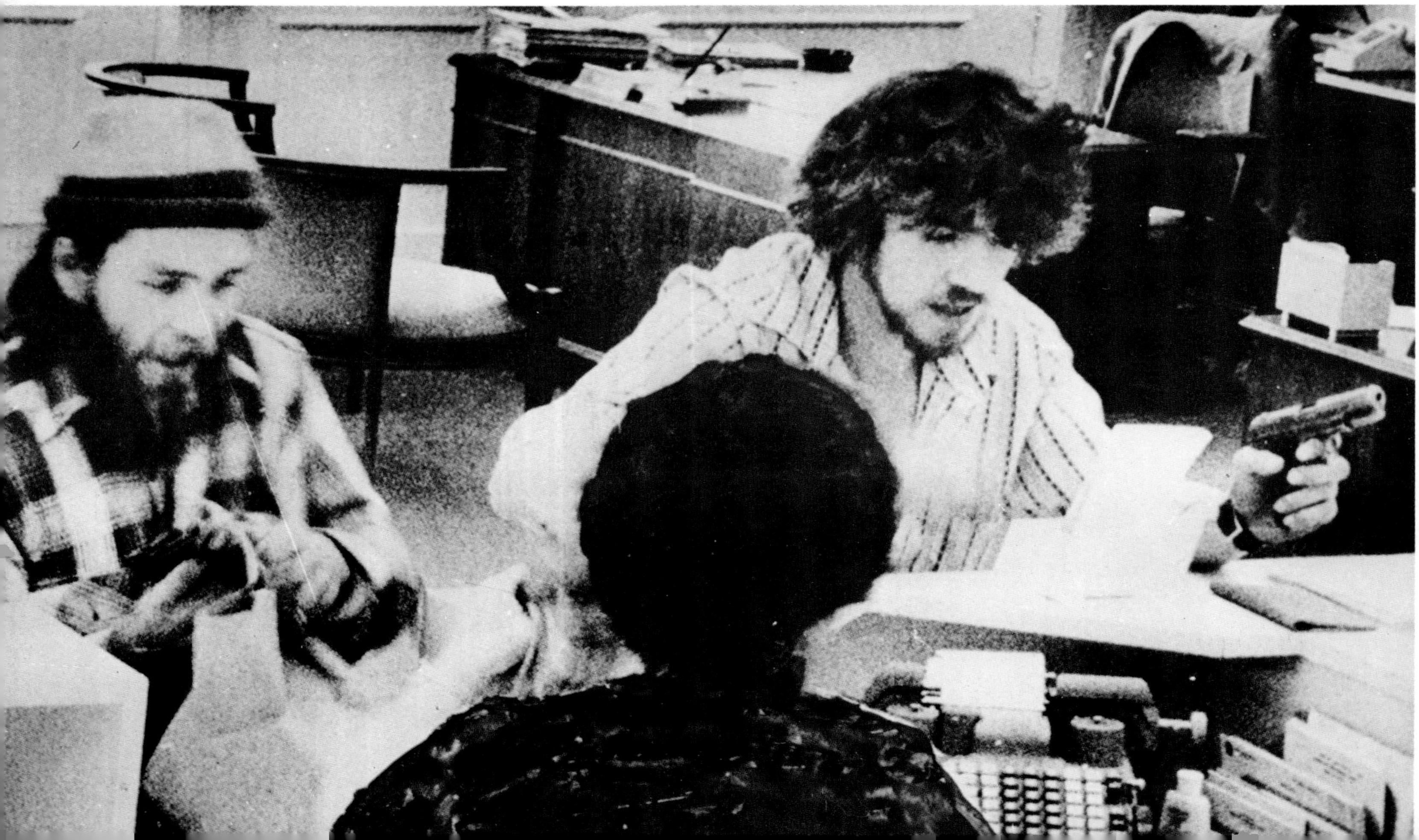

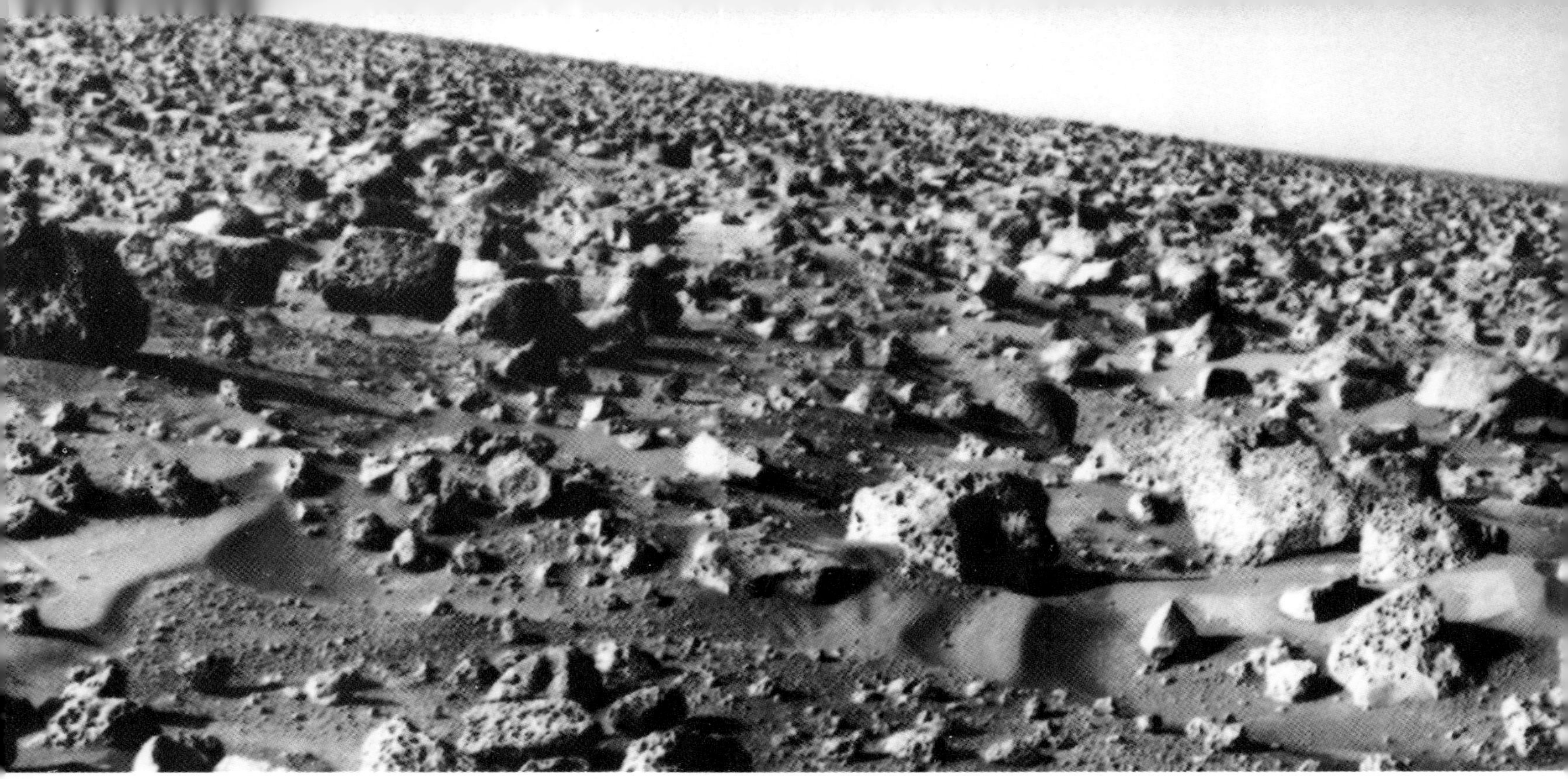

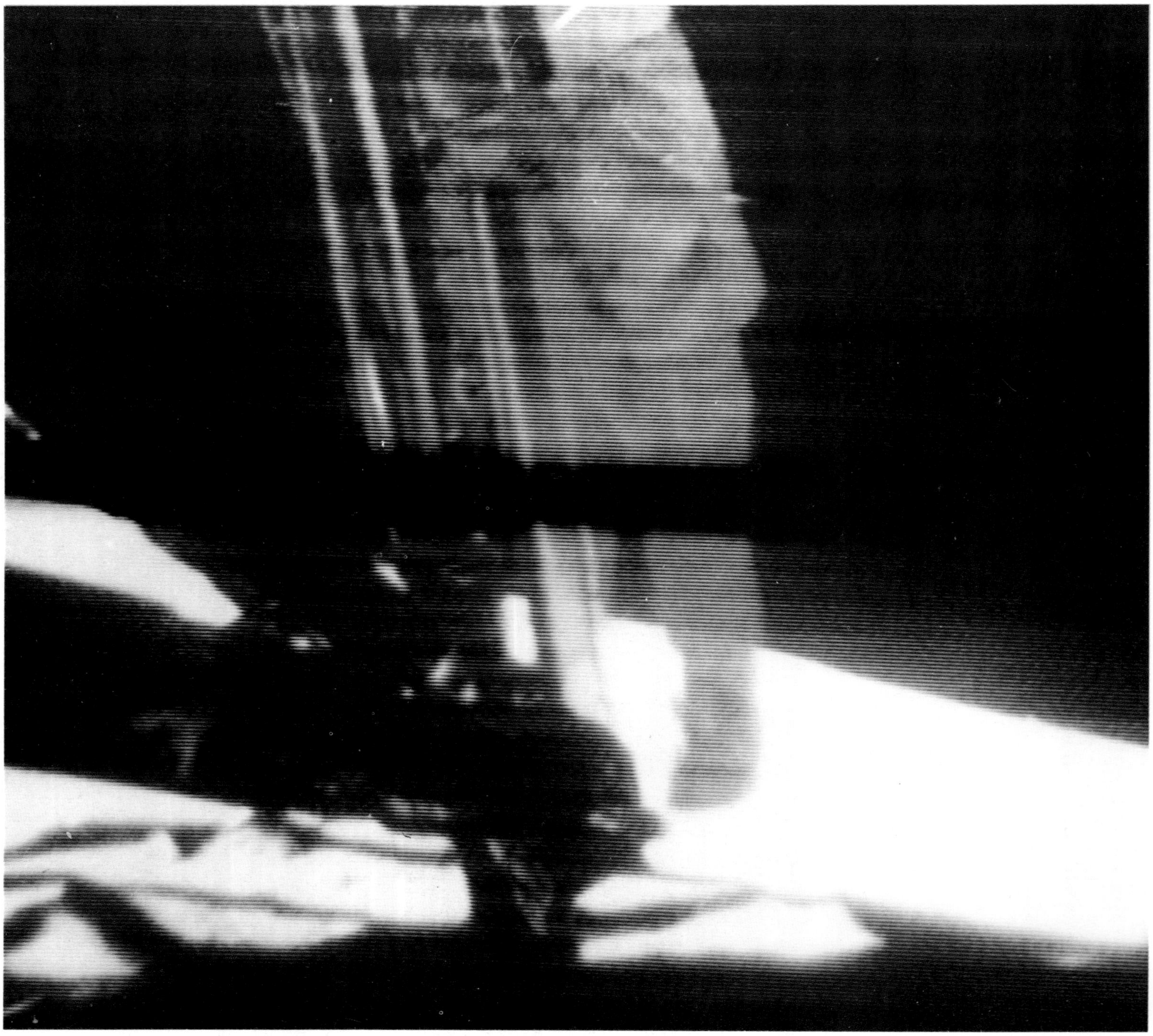

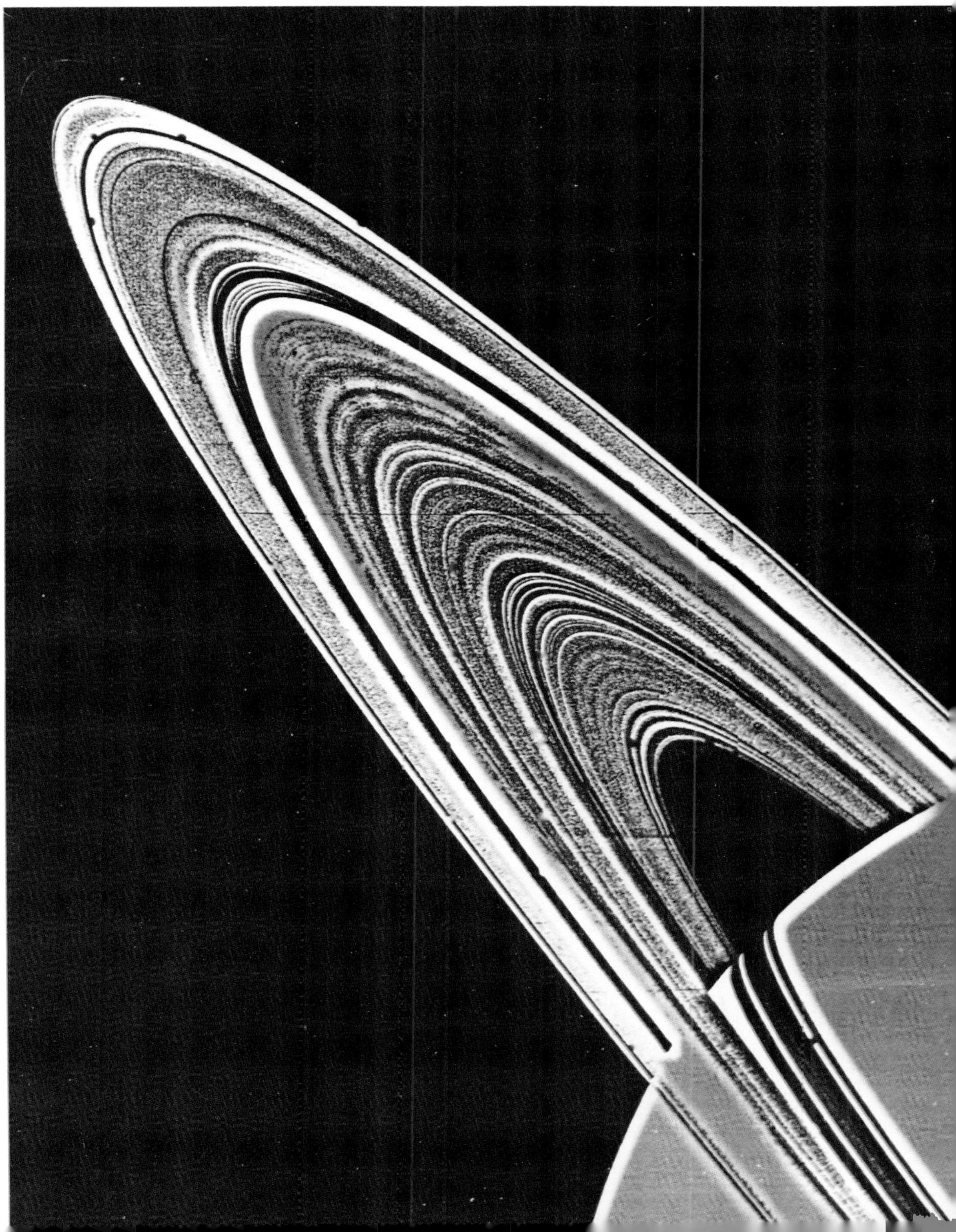

At the distant extreme of automated picture-taking was the photographic record of man's exploration of space.

Astronaut Neil Armstrong's "small step" on to the surface of the moon on July 20, 1969—mankind's first—was relayed to earth as electronic data and received at the Jet Propulsion Laboratory in Pasadena, Calif. The black area across the center was caused by a malfunction in the television ground data handling system at the tracking station.

The picture of Armstrong dangling his left leg as he stood on the lunar lander was taken a moment before he stepped on the surface. Later, he and fellow astronaut Edwin Aldrin set up a camera away from the spacecraft.

Computerized cameras made the long trip to Mars, too—without any human company.

The Viking 2 robot lander carried a camera that took this 85-degree panorama sweeping across the plain on Mars in September 1976. With the camera mounted on a turret atop the lander, it beamed its view back to the JPL, one thin vertical strip at a time. Even at the speed of light, it was a 20-minute trip.

The computer-assembled two-image mosaic of Saturn's rings was taken by NASA's Voyager 1 on Nov. 6, 1980—from a distance of five million miles.

Sometimes, the human eye is not enough.

Attempted Coup

"Everybody quiet! Everybody down to the floor!"

The orders were accompanied by a burst of gunfire inside the Spanish parliament on Feb. 23, 1981.

It was to have been the day for the confirmation of an orderly transfer of rule from Adolfo Suarez, who had resigned, to Leopoldo Calvo Sotelo, who had been nominated as the new premier. But, as the members of the lower house were casting their votes that afternoon, civil guard members of a right-wing military faction stormed into the hall with submachine guns at the ready.

Led by Lt. Col. Antonio Tejero Molina, pictured here brandishing a pistol, the guards held the 350 Cabinet members and legislators as hostages for 18 hours in the attempted coup before surrendering.

Quake Disaster

A mother wailed in front of the dead bodies of all her five children.

A 2-year-old boy and his 5-year-old sister stood in the rubble that once was their home. Their parents were nowhere to be found.

These were the tragic scenes of death and destruction left by a devastating earthquake in eastern Turkey on Oct. 30, 1983. The tremors were felt in mountainous provinces bordering Iran, Syria and Iraq.

The death toll was 1,332. More than 10,000 children were left homeless. Worst hit was the village of Muratbagi, where these photographs were taken. Nearly 50 were killed in Muratbagi alone.

The mud-brick and stone village houses of the region easily collapse in a quake. The eastern area sits atop an earthquake-prone belt known as the Anatolian fault.

In this century, quakes claimed 70,000 lives in Turkey.

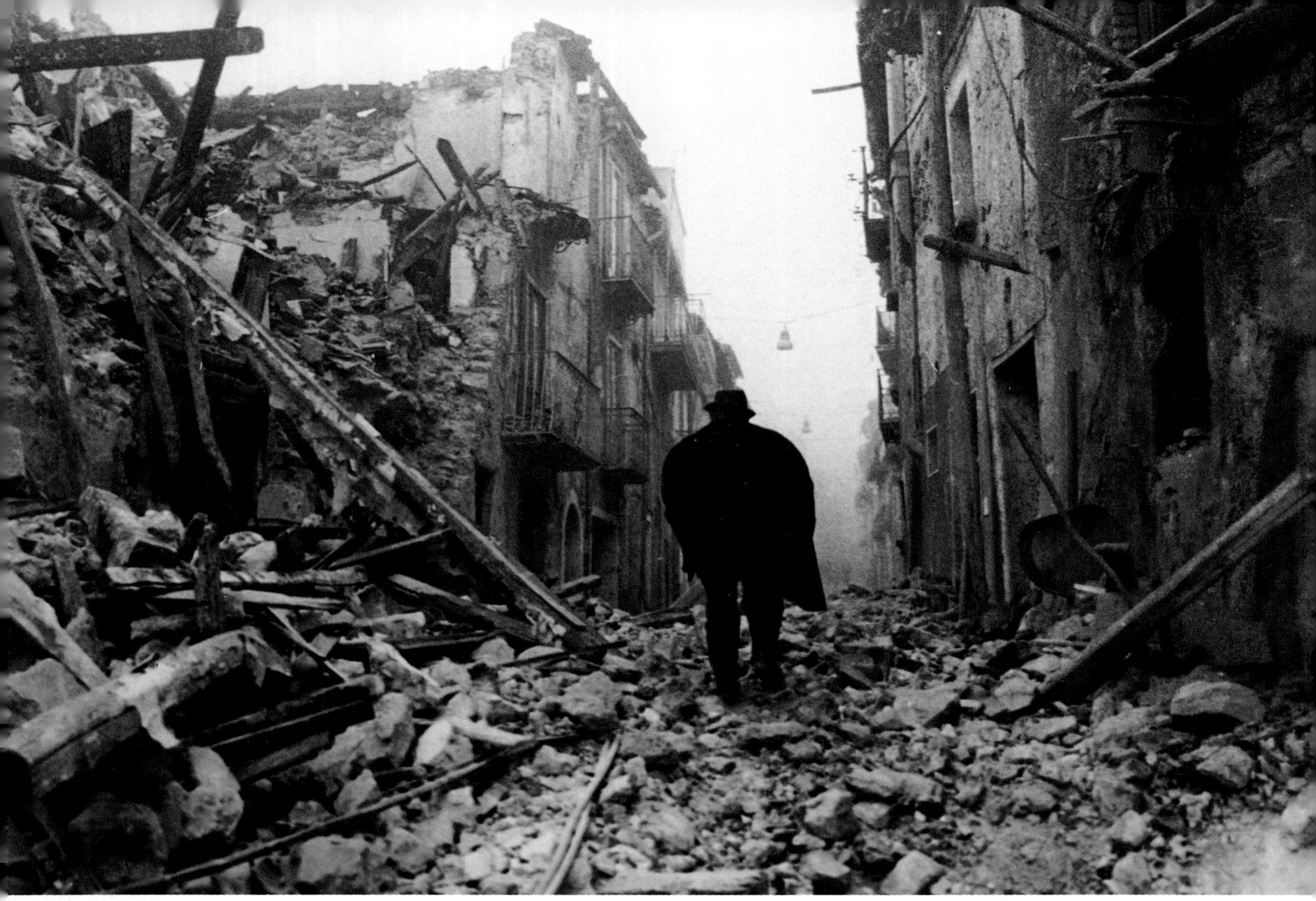

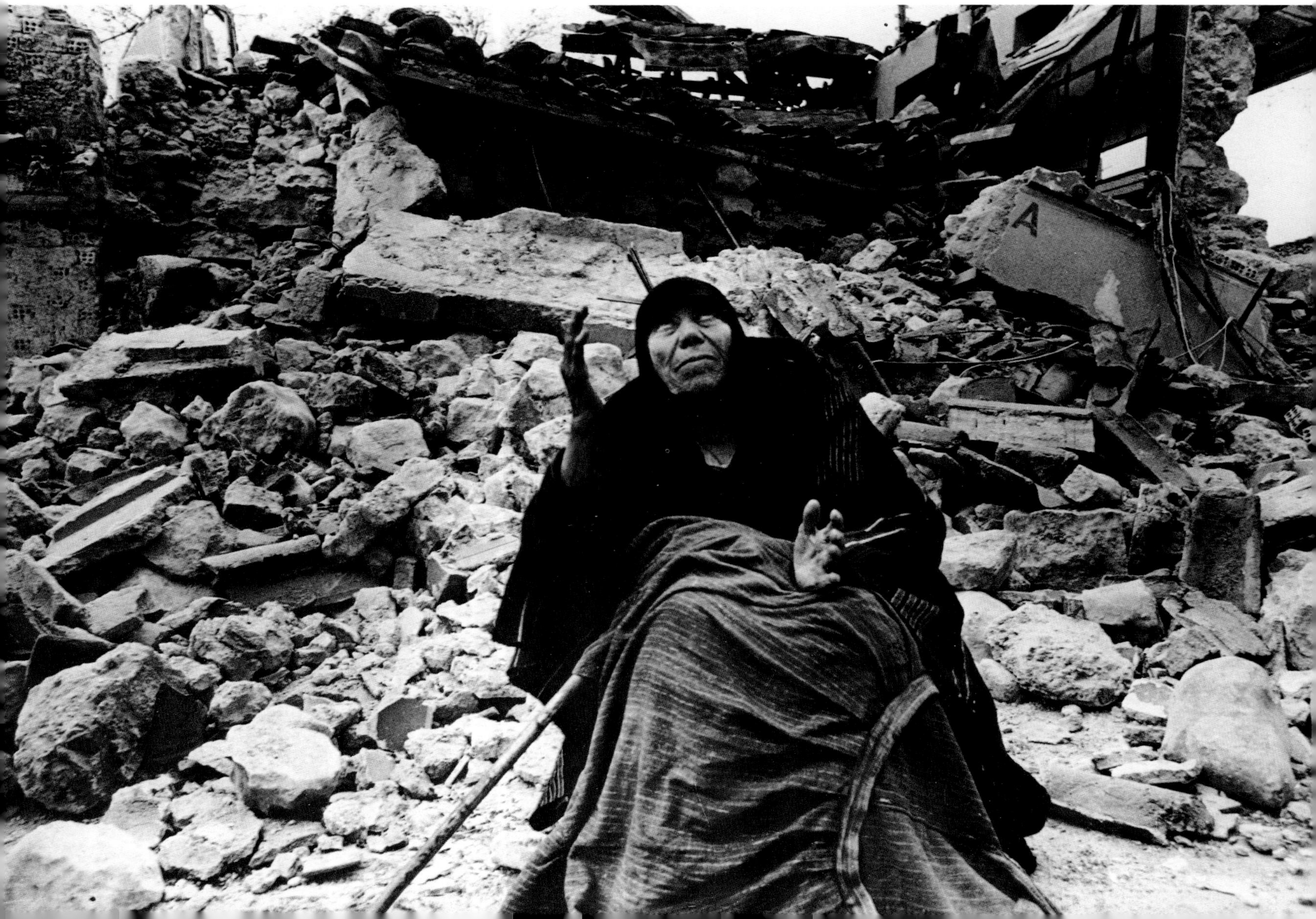

"...The Earth Opened..."

"... The ground did cleave asunder that was under them. And the earth opened her mouth, and swallowed them up, and their households . . ."

From the Bible to the heart-rending reality experienced all too often over the centuries. A lone man walking amid the debris underscored the devastation of an earthquake in southern Italy in 1980. An old woman looked skyward in prayer after her village in Greece was virtually swallowed up in 1981.

Squatters Scattered

Modderdam, in Afrikaans, means "muddy dam."

It was the appropriate name of a squatter's camp of about 1,000 shanties on the outskirts of Cape Town, South Africa, where blacks must live in segregated townships.

In August 1977, the South African government set out to demolish the camp, and others like it, ruling that the blacks were squatting illegally and that a lack of water or sanitary conditions constituted health hazards.

When a crowd of hundreds of blacks singing hymns in their native Xhosa protested the demolition of their housing, police fired tear gas at them. This photo, "Teargas Terror," earned a World Press Photo award for Leslie Hammond of the Argus Press, Cape Town.

A government bulldozer later finished the demolition.

Volcanic Deathscape

It was a clear, sunny Sunday morning in Vancouver in southwest Washington state. Some 40 miles away loomed Mount St. Helens, a snow-capped 9,677-foot peak that had been threatening for months to blow its top.

At 8:32 a.m. on May 18, 1980, it did.

Two quick earthquakes shook the mountain and broke off a blister of ice and rock that had been bulging from its north slope. Suddenly, a wall of rock where the bulge had been blew out with a force of 10 million tons of TNT — releasing energy pent up since its last eruption more than 100 years before.

The eruption blew ash 13 miles in the air, dusted cities and farms in four states and twisted the surrounding 150 square miles into a deathscape.

The unstoppable flow of ash and rock slides and mudflows left 57 people dead or missing.

Photos by George Wedding, San Jose Mercury News.

Odd Sport

Sports events offer vicarious excitement, thrills, agonies, ecstasies—and, from certain photo perspectives, laughs.

The relay runner set for a start may be thinking he has to be faster than a speeding bullet to finish this race, but it's only a distortion caused by camera lens foreshortening.

The baseball umpire seems to be doing a unique balancing act, but again it's all in the lens angle.

Even the Houston Rockets basketball player appears to be using his head to advantage, but it's only passing fancy.

On the other hand, the high school golfer seems to have lost his head during an invitational tournament.

Pope Shot

This startling photograph spots a gun in the hand of a would-be assassin aiming at Pope John Paul II.

The pope had just finished circling the Vatican's St. Peter's Square on a slow-moving jeep, en route to his weekly general audience before 15,000 tourists and faithful.

It was shortly after 5 p.m. May 13, 1981, when the shots rang out.

A terrible quiet fell over the crowd, followed by sudden screams and yelling. The pope slumped over. Blood stained his white robe.

Security agents quickly picked up the 60-year-old pontiff and rushed him by car to a hospital where he underwent surgery and blood transfusions for 5½ hours.

He recovered.

Police arrested Mehmet Ali Agca, a Turk, who had vowed to kill the pope after he had escaped from an Istanbul prison in 1979. Agca was later sentenced to life in prison.

At Christmas in 1983, the pope visited him in his prison cell and personally pardoned him, though that had no legal import.

They call him a "forejumper" —a skier who tests the track before the official competition begins.

Mark Johnson, of Duluth, Minn., accepted the challenge for the Winter Olympics at Lake Placid, N.Y., in 1980.

This sequence of photographs by Mitsunori Chigita follows Johnson off the 70-meter jump, his loss of balance in the air, and, finally, his tumble into the snow.

Storybook Victory

With fans rhythmically cheering "U-S-A, U-S-A, U-S-A," the United States Olympic hockey team stunned the athletic world by winning the 1980 gold medal at Lake Placid, N.Y.

At the top of the list of thrilling victories by the Cinderella, come-from-behind team — which was not considered a strong contender for any medal at the start of the Games — was a 4-3 triumph over the Soviet Union, a team that had not lost a game in Olympic competition in a dozen years.

Two days later, the Americans defeated Finland, 4-2, to assure the gold.

AP photographer Dave Tenenbaum was at both games, catching the storybook excitement of the final triumph in the picture of goalie Jim Craig standing on the ice draped in the American flag.

Falklands Fireball

"She came slowly up the bay, making smoke, a main mast bent over at an angle. There were holes along her sides.

"About a half-hour after dark, there was an explosion aboard. A fire started amidships and spread swiftly from the waterline to the deck. . . . There were more explosions. They sent flames high into the air as the ship burned white hot through the night.

"On the deck near me, small knots of men looked on in horror as the ship died."

So British Broadcasting Corp. Correspondent Brian Hanrahan described the sinking of the British frigate Antelope after a 500-pound bomb lodged in its engine room blew up on May 24, 1982.

The bomb was dropped by Argentine warplanes over San Carlos Bay in the Falkland Islands. A bomb disposal expert trying to defuse the bomb was killed and seven other sailors were wounded.

The dramatic photograph of the huge fireball ripping through the Antelope was taken by Press Association staff photographer Martin Cleaver, with the task force at Port San Carlos off East Falkland.

The war between Britain and Argentina over the right to rule the Falkland Islands lasted 74 days before the Argentine forces surrendered on June 14.

Enmity Becomes Amity

For centuries, since Moses led his people out of the pharaoh's land, they were Semitic cousins, but blood enemies.

Since the modern establishment of the state of Israel in 1948, there had been a state of war. There seemed no end to the enmity.

Then, Egypt stepped away from the Arab fold in an attempt to establish peace with its Israeli neighbor.

First, Egyptian President Anwar Sadat went to Israel in November 1977, a daring step for an Arab leader. That historic trip started the process leading to a peace treaty. U.S. President Jimmy Carter served as the peace-maker between Sadat and Israeli Prime Minister Menachem Begin in the up-and-down negotiations in Washington, D.C., and Camp David, Md. The talks finally ended in agreement between the two Middle East nations.

The formal peace treaty was signed at the White House in Washington on March 26, 1979.

On that chilly early spring day, an emotional Prime Minister Begin said: "No more war, no more bloodshed, no more bereavement. Peace unto you, shalom, salaam, forever."

President Sadat paraphrased the Biblical text: "Let us work together until the day comes when they beat their swords into plowshares and their spears into pruning hooks."

After 30 years of war, the peaceful promise of the future appeared in the smiles of the three world leaders clasping hands after the signing ceremony.

Parade of Death

Just before it happened, President Anwar Sadat of Egypt was laughing heartily with his top advisers. They were on the reviewing stand as thousands of the nation's soldiers marched by that Oct. 6, 1981, commemorating the eighth anniversary of the Yom Kippur War against Israel.

Just after 1 p.m., six Egyptian air force jet fighters thundered over the reviewing stand, trailing red, blue, white and yellow smoke.

Most of the spectators were watching the jets when the occasion turned to bloody disaster in a matter of minutes.

Six Egyptian soldiers jumped from a truck in the military parade and charged, firing automatic weapons and throwing grenades as they raced about 20 yards from the parade roadway to the three-foot-high reviewing stand.

Bloodied dignitaries were thrown into pandemonium by the attack. The stand was quickly littered with the dead and wounded, bullet-ridden armchairs adding to the gruesome scene.

President Sadat, whose peace with Israel changed the course of Middle East policy, was killed. The assassins were identified as Moslem fundamentalists. Five others were killed and some two score wounded.

The photos are by AP staffer Bill Foley and El Koussy, Sygma.

Presidential Quartet

In an unusual occurrence, four presidents of the United States are pictured together on the South Lawn of the White House. The occasion was President Reagan's announcement of sympathy for slain Egyptian President Anwar Sadat in October 1981. Reagan is flanked by Gerald Ford and Richard Nixon on the left, Jimmy Carter on the right, with Nancy Reagan behind him. The three former presidents represented the United States at Sadat's funeral in Cairo.

"Pop! Pop!...Pop! Pop! Pop! Pop!"

BULLETIN
WASHINGTON (AP)—Several gunshots were fired at President Reagan as he left a downtown Washington hotel today.

Gunshots fired at the president. It sounded all too terrifyingly familiar

It was 2:25 p.m. March 30, 1981. President Reagan had just finished speaking to the Building and Construction Trades Department of the AFL-CIO at the Washington Hilton Hotel. He was leaving the hotel through the VIP side entrance. His limousine was a few feet away.

Reporters and photographers were outside waiting for him. So was John W. Hinckley.

"Pop! Pop! . . . Pop! Pop! Pop! Pop!" AP White House Correspondent Mike Putzel was standing just short of the right taillight of the president's car.

"Gunshots. Had to be," Putzel later recalled. "But the

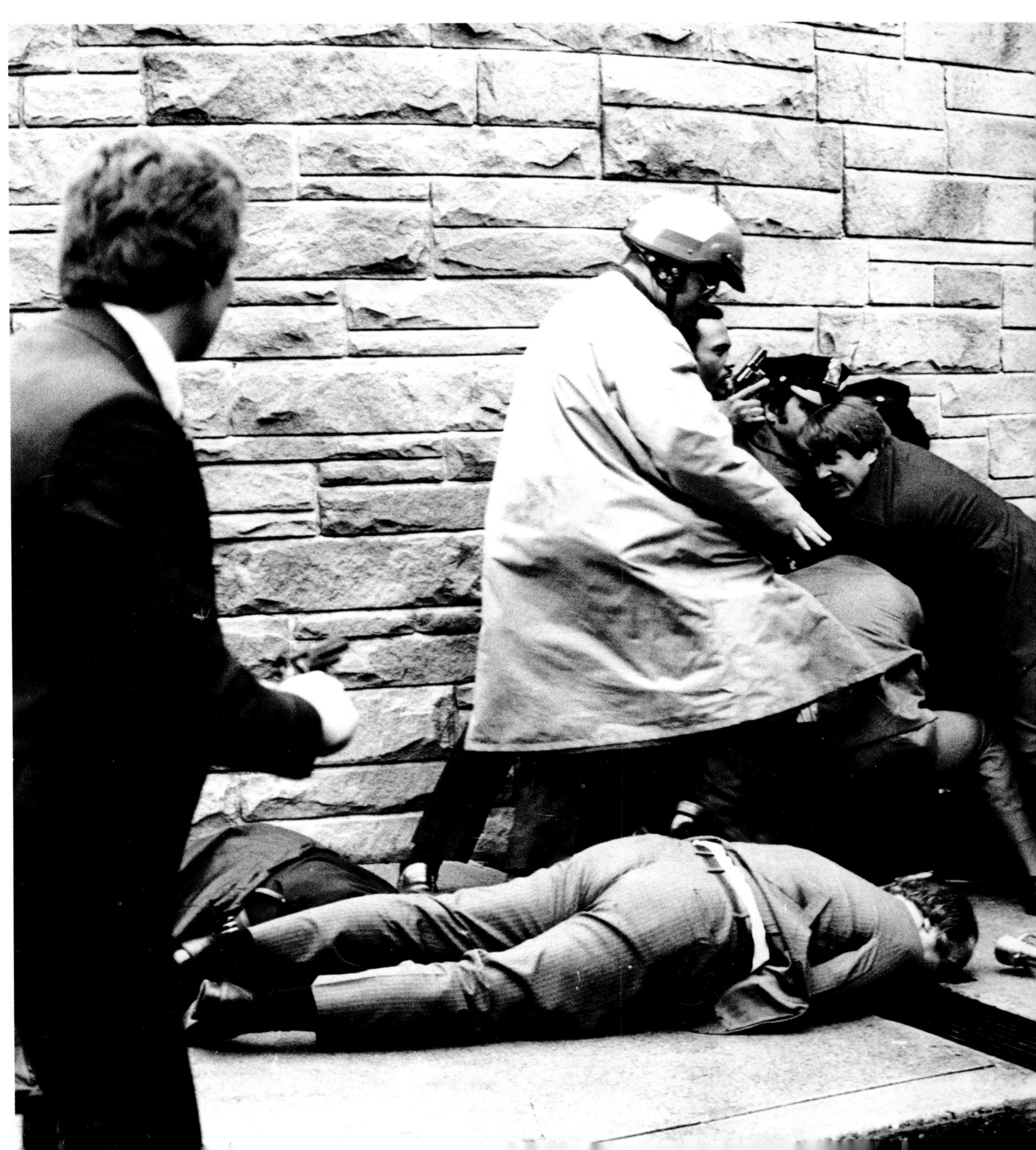

sound was ricocheting off the stone wall next to us. A scuffle developed a few steps to my right. I learned later that's where the would-be assassin was standing. . . ."

Photographer Ron Edmonds, an AP staff man only a month and on his second day of duty at the White House, was standing on the other side of Reagan's car.

"As he approached the limousine waving first to his right and then to his left, I clicked my first frame," Edmonds remembered.

"I heard a 'pop' and saw him react. I kept the shutter down on my motorized camera and continued shooting frames as Secret Service agents pushed the president into the car. . . .

"As the limousine moved out I swung to my right and

started making pictures of the gunman being wrestled to the ground. It was then that I spotted the three wounded men on the ground. That's when I first realized that what I had heard was gunfire."

The sequence won a Pulitzer Prize for Edmonds.

Reagan "sailed through surgery" that removed a bullet from his left lung.

The three others hit were a Secret Service agent, a policeman and presidential press secretary James Brady. Brady, shot in the head, underwent extensive surgery and rehabilitation and remained partially paralyzed.

John W. Hinckley, 25-year-old would-be assassin, was tried and found not guilty by reason of insanity and committed to the government asylum at St. Elizabeths.

Air Collision

It was the final heat of the last race on the last day of the National Airways midget air races in Frederick, Md., in 1966.

Photographer Robert Walker took advantage of a Civil Air Patrol offer to ride up in a photo plane. When both planes came into his viewfinder, he started snapping through a 500mm lens. He caught the moment of impact and saw the parts strewn about the air.

The pilot of one plane landed in a cornfield — and walked away, unhurt. The other was only slightly injured.

Icy Rescue

"I had a pretty good indication things weren't going right when we started down the runway . . . that we did not have takeoff speed. I knew we were out of runway."

Passenger Joe Stiley recalled the moments before Air Florida Flight 90, headed out of Washington National Airport that snowy Jan. 13, 1982, and crashed into a nearby Potomac River bridge.

The jetliner smashed cars on the bridge and then plunged beneath the icy waters of the Potomac.

Seventy-four of the plane's 79 passengers and crew members were killed, along with four people in vehicles on the bridge.

In initial rescue efforts, police and military helicopters lowered life rings to survivors in the river.

People clung to pieces of the airplane in the water, grabbed for lifelines lowered from the bridge or thrown out by rescuers on the ice. Rescuers used sticks, paddles, anything that might work, to help survivors get to shore.

Lenny Skutnik was one of the rescuers who succeeded. He was on shore and saw a woman trying to reach land. She was clinging to a rope.

"I felt so helpless," he remembered. "I couldn't do anything... She just gave out. I jerked off my coat and my boots and dove in."

He grabbed her just as she started to go under.

These photos, taken from an ABC-TV© monitor, show a Park Service helicopter pulling in one victim of the crash and Skutnik rescuing passenger Priscilla Tirado, who suffered a broken leg.

Pasture in White

Dual board fences and a herd of standardbred horses on a farm in southeastern Pennsylvania provide the contrast to a field of white. Jim Gerberich took the picture for the Lancaster New Era in January 1984.

Processions

The death of a national leader brings grieving and mourning—and then the spotlight shifts to the successor.

The funeral processions of these Soviet leaders had much to tell about the political procession.

When Josef Stalin's coffin was carried out of the House of Trade Unions in Moscow in 1953, the pallbearers were, in the front, left to right: Georgi Malenkov, Vassily Stalin, V.M. Molotov, Marshal Bulganin, Lazar Kaganovich, Nikolai Shvernik, and on the extreme right of the front, Lavrenti Beria. (Photo: Tass from Sovfoto.) Malenkov became the premier, but was forced out in 1955 and replaced by Bulganin who was dismissed in 1958 when Nikita Khrushchev became premier as well as Communist Party chairman.

At the funeral of Leonid Brezhnev (who came to power after Khrushchev) in 1982, the pallbearers included Yuri Andropov (with glasses in foreground) and Konstantin Chernenko (second to right of Andropov). (Photo: Tass from Sovfoto.)

Andropov became premier.
At his funeral in February 1984, Chernenko led those carrying the coffin to the Kremlin Wall—and became premier.

Massacre in Lebanon

The conflict in the Middle East runs long and deep — through religious, cultural and political animosity and into irrational hate.

No diplomatic or military efforts have been able to solve it, or even ease it. The embers seem to glow perpetually, flaring now and again into open conflict.

In 1982, the frustrations and hatred in the region exploded into yet another tragic example of man's inhumanity to man.

On June 6, Israeli forces had invaded Lebanon, intending to drive Palestinian guerrillas out of the southern portion of the nation, whence they had terrorized Jewish villages. By July 30, Israeli troops had West Beirut surrounded and insisted that the guerrillas leave the city. They were gone by Sept. 3; U.S. Marines left soon after.

On Sept. 14, newly-elected President Bashir Gemayel was assassinated and Israeli troops invaded West Beirut, besieging the Palestinian refugee camps, Sabra and Shatila, in the southern outskirts. On the next day, Lebanese Christian militias were sighted with Israeli troops in the southern suburbs.

Soon, reports began to spread of a massacre of Palestinian civilians in the refugee camps.

"We knew there was something going on in the camps," AP photographer Bill Foley recalled, "but were prevented from entering by militiamen at the entrance. I could hear sporadic arms fire in the distance."

After two more fruitless attempts, Foley returned to Sabra a third time, with AP reporter G.G. LaBelle.

"There was no one guarding the entrance, only a very strange quiet. We entered and discovered that we were seeing the aftermath of a massacre that had ended only minutes before.

"Everywhere there was death—dead men, women and children. The stench of death was overpowering. . . .

"I will never forget those days in the camps. Women wailing at the discovery of bodies of their family and friends. The surreal funeral services. The ability of human beings to inflict incredible suffering on others. It will always be with me."

For his pictures of the victims and survivors of the massacre, Foley earned the Pulitzer Prize in 1983.

The photos show an elderly Palestinian woman brandishing two militiamen helmets that she said were worn by those who massacred her countrymen; two Palestinian women weeping after finding the bodies of relatives killed; a Lebanese civilian bicyclist riding through the camp, passing two of the hundreds of corpses.

Beirut Blast

The day broke sunny and warm. Inside the glass and concrete building where the Marines slept, only the cooks were stirring. It was 6:20 a.m. on Sunday, Oct. 23, 1983.

The Marines of the U.S. peace-keeping force were in their barracks at Beirut International Airport. Many of them never awoke.

A red pickup truck wheeled into the airport parking lot behind the building, then speeded up and smashed through a steel gate. It crashed through two other metal barricades and careened around a third.

Nothing stopped it.

The suicide truck kept going toward the four-story building, burst through a layer of sandbags and came to a halt in the lobby. There, its cargo of some 2,000 pounds of explosives went off with a roar that turned a quiet dawn into a day of horror.

The building collapsed into a heap of rubble. Glass flew everywhere; doors were blown off their hinges.

Photos by Hussein Ammar and AP staffer Bill Foley show the rescue work that went on for days in a frantic search for survivors.

When the body count was done, 240 had died, dozens more in a similar bombing at a French encampment not far away.

Only six months before, Foley had photographed the aftermath of the bombing of the U.S. Embassy in Beirut.

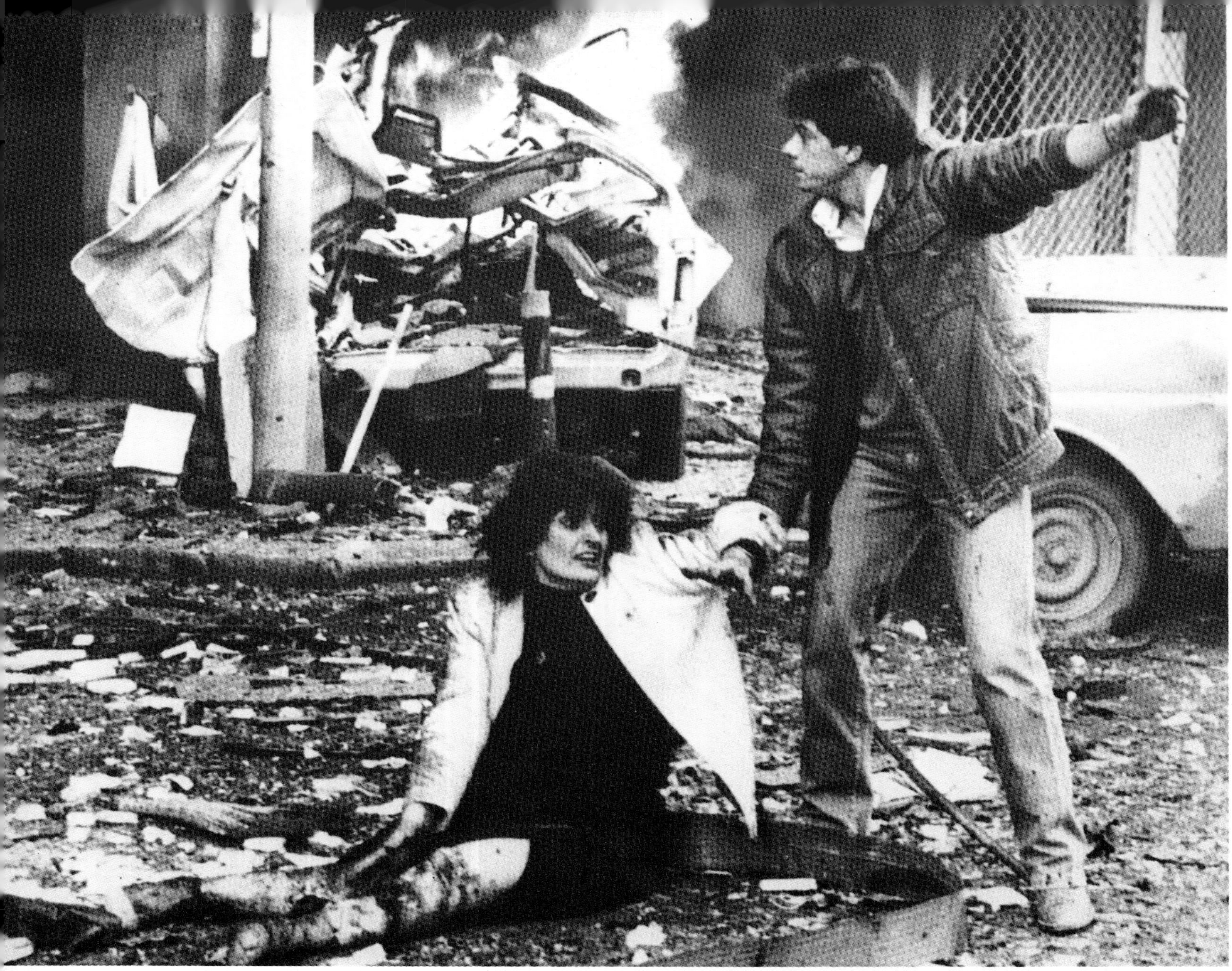

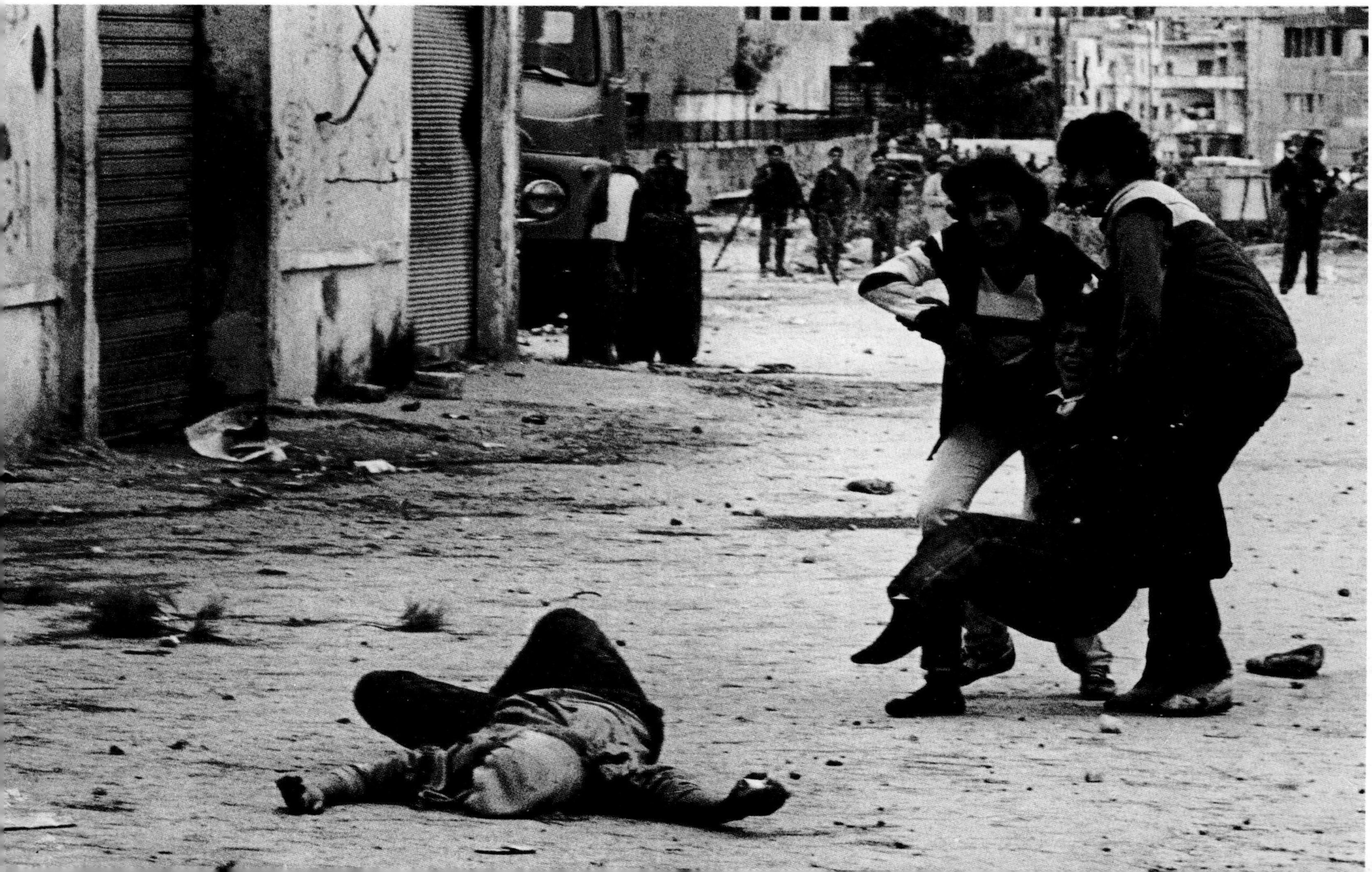

Victims

Grief, the poet said, is a tree that has tears for its fruit.

In Lebanon, an elderly man wiped a tear from his eye during a memorial service for victims of the massacre in Beirut in 1982 . . .

A woman wept as she held a photo of her lost child . . .

A rescue worker pulled a wounded woman from the wreckage of a bombed building in Beirut; at least eight were killed, more than 50 wounded, scores trapped.

A woman lay wounded on the ground after being hit by small arms fire in Sidon, Lebanon; her hysterical friend is carried away from the scene . . .

The victims are not only those who die.

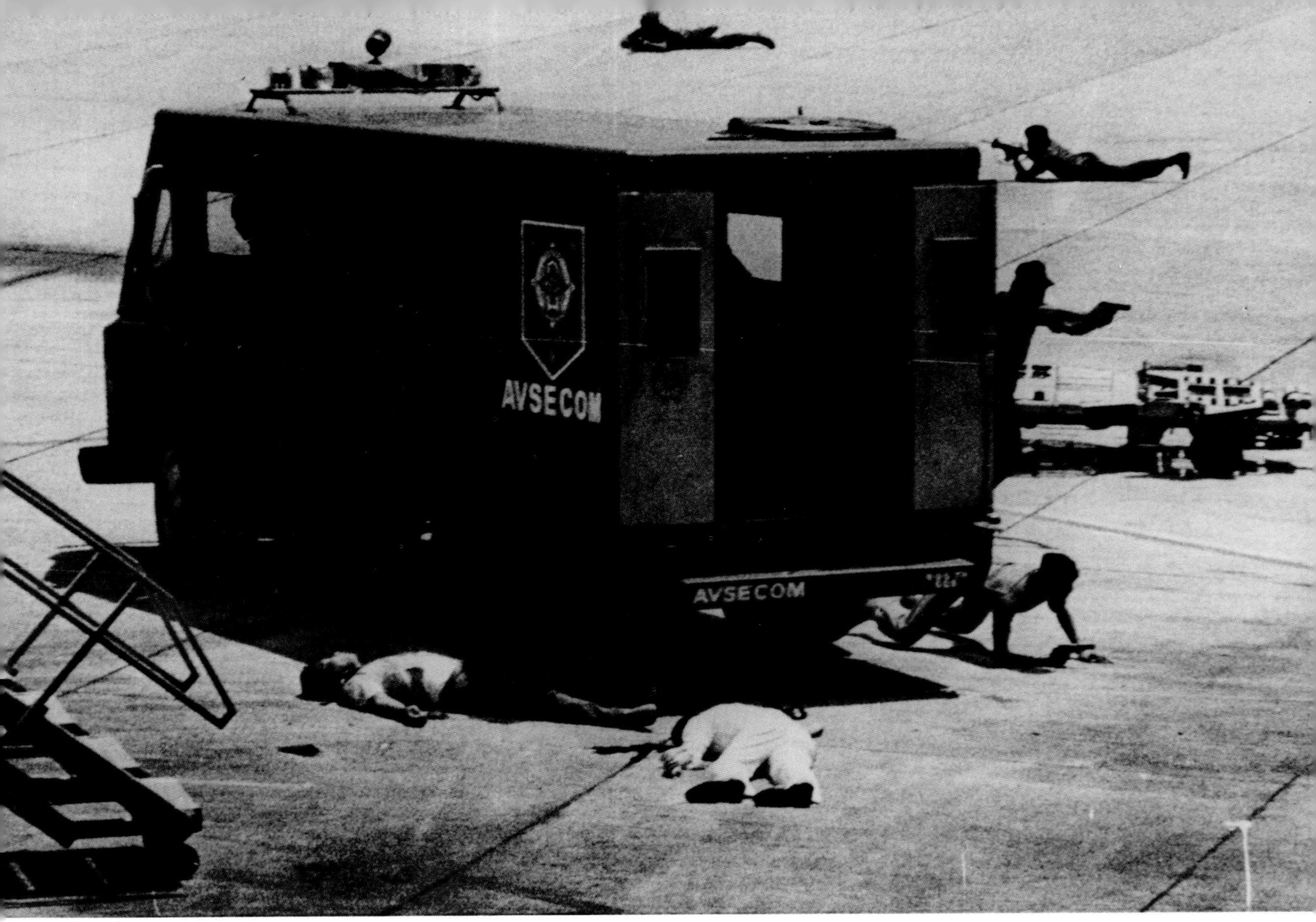
AVSECOM
AVSECOM

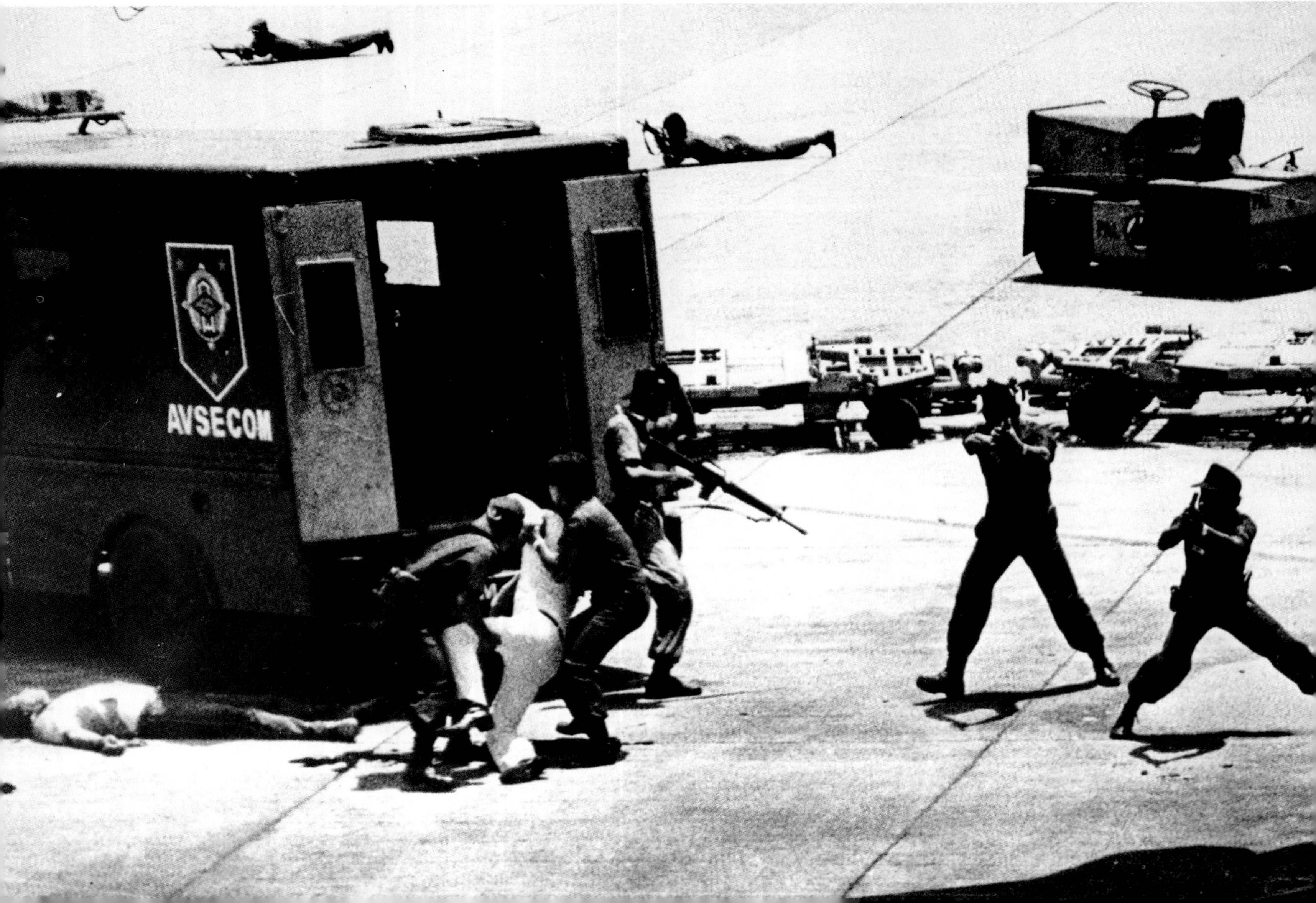
AVSECOM

Aquino Assassinated

Benigno Aquino Jr. was coming home to the Philippines after three years of self-exile in the United States.

He was aware of the danger he faced, but he said he could not let fear of assassination prevent him from returning. "It's my feeling that we all have to die sometime," he said aboard the plane. "If it is my place to die from an assassin's bullet, so be it."

As opposition leader to the government of President Ferdinand Marcos, the former Filipino senator felt "I have to suffer with my people. I have to lead them."

As he stepped off the China Airlines flight at Manila International Airport on Aug. 21, 1983, he was killed by a single gunshot in the back of the head.

Airport security men carried his body into a security van after killing his assassin, whose body lies on the ground at the left of the van. He was later identified as Rolando Galman.

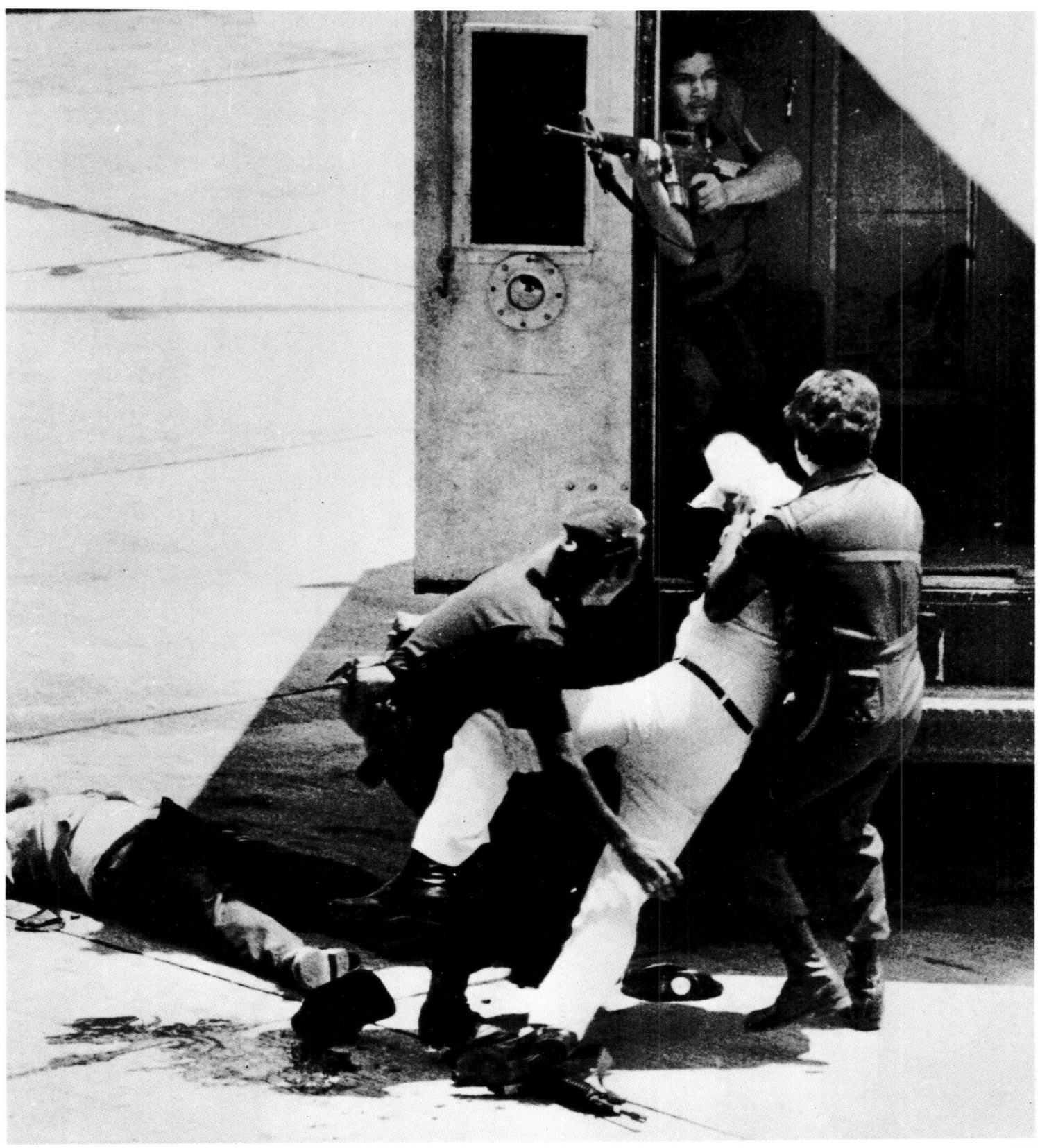

Death Leap

"I have nothing to live for."

That's what police said Ralph Garcia told them as he prepared to leap from an upper Manhattan overpass that Saturday, Aug. 23, 1982. Policemen could not talk him out of it, but tried to move a giant air bag to the spot where he would land.

This startling sequence of pictures by AP photographer Ron Frehm shows the distraught man talking with police, then jumping some 50 feet to the pavement below.

Police Sgt. Charles Gunther said the man "deliberately tried to miss the air bag—and did."

He died on impact.

Crash Weekend

Daytona Beach in Florida has long been a mecca of speed racing, its long, sweeping oceanfront of sand having first been used for auto sports as far back as 1900. In 1936, the racing was limited to stock cars, with the beach used as one straightaway and a blacktop road for another, with turns cut through sand dunes to connect them.

Eventually, it became the Daytona International Speedway, home of the 500-mile race for stock cars. It is there that on Friday night, Saturday or Sunday of a "Speedweek," the hell-for-leather drivers, mechanics, car owners, friends and thrill-seekers move to the track.

On this one weekend in February 1984, there was more than watching for a winner that caused concern among spectators and racers alike.

Chevrolets driven by Steve Moore (No. 73) and Bobby Wawak (74) collided during the first run of two 125-mile qualifying races.

Rookie driver Randy La Joie in his Chevrolet (No. 07) hit an inside wall during the second qualifying

run and rebounded, upside down, then vertical, with parts flying out.

A fireman was hit by a car traveling backwards in the pits as crew members and spectators scrambled to safety.

And in another fiery crash, a Buick driven by Natz Peters (No. 60) collided with Jim Hurlbert's Buick during a consolation race for drivers who failed to qualify.

Purrfect Fall

It was Be Kind to Animals Week in Pennsylvania. Fate was kind to the 5-week-old kitten brought along for the proclamation signings in the reception room of Gov. Dick Thornburgh.

Eric Hendrik of the Pennsylvania Society for the Prevention of Cruelty to Animals reached to catch the falling kitten as the governor reacted somewhat apprehensively. The kitten landed on its paws, unhurt.

Points and Counterpoint

There were four seconds remaining in the game; the Stanford Cardinals had just gone ahead of California, 20-19, that Nov. 23, 1982.

Stanford's ensuing kickoff was caught by Kevin Moen at the 45 yard line. He passed it back to Richard Rodgers, who then flipped it to Dwight Garner, who was grabbed by two Stanford tacklers. Many thought the play was over then; Stanford substitutes came out on the field — and so did both bands, from each end zone.

But the play went on. Garner lateraled to Rodgers who then lateraled to Marriet Ford — who passed it back to Moen, who started it all. Moen ran in for the winning touchdown.

Five laterals on one play. Doesn't that just beat the band?

Photo by Bob Stinnett, Oakland Tribune.

Averting a Jump

It must have all seemed too much for Steven T. Wougamon, an accused killer and racketeer.

So he stepped out on the ledge of the Federal Courts Building in St. Louis in the freezing temperatures of December 1983.

Officials spent almost an hour talking with him before he came in from the cold.

Photographer Joan Toeniskoetter followed the ordeal through to its safe conclusion.

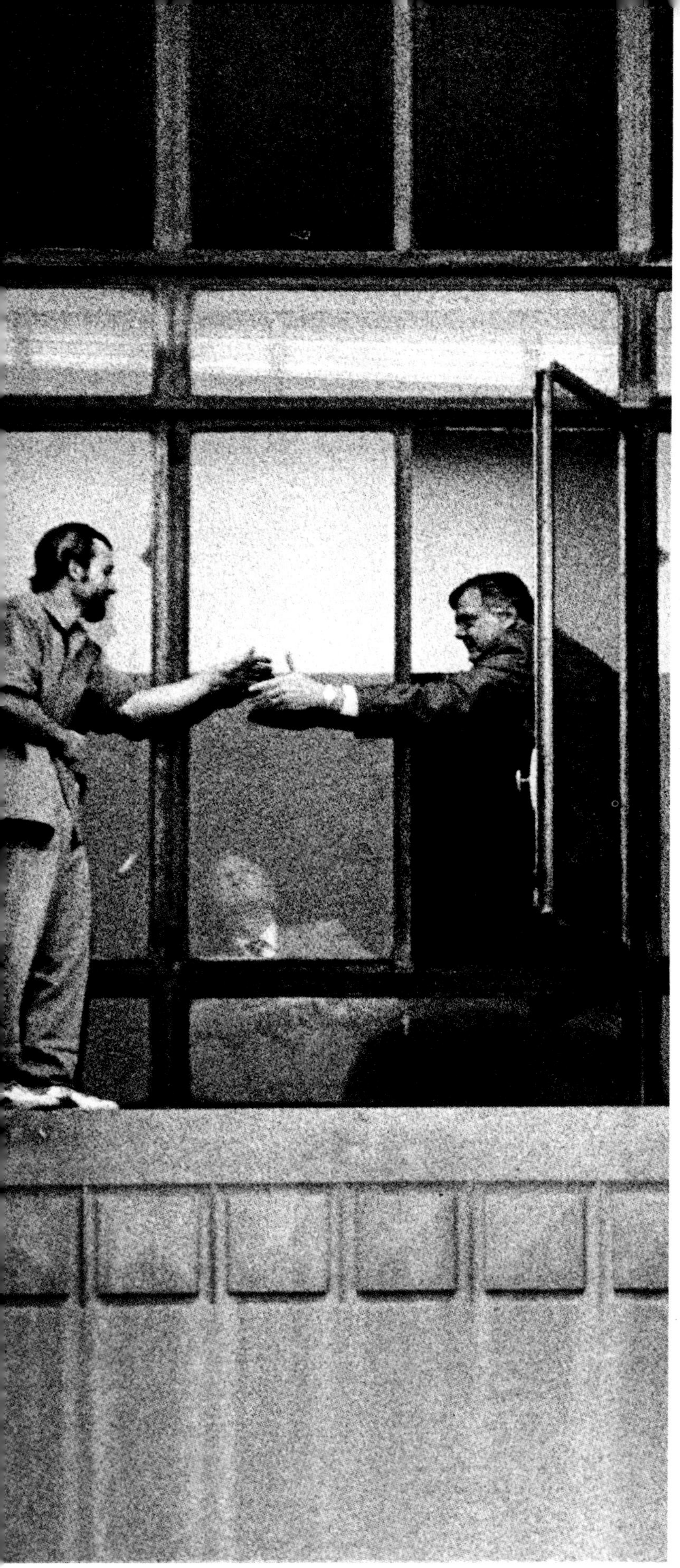
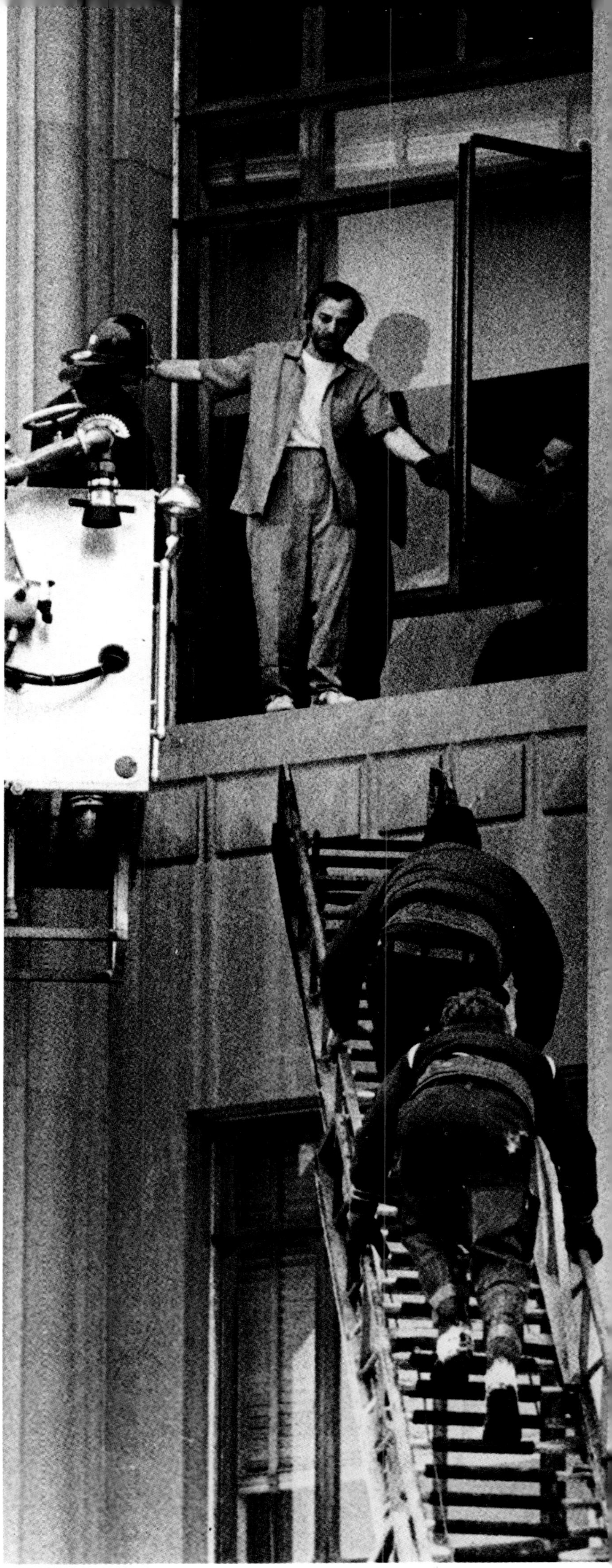

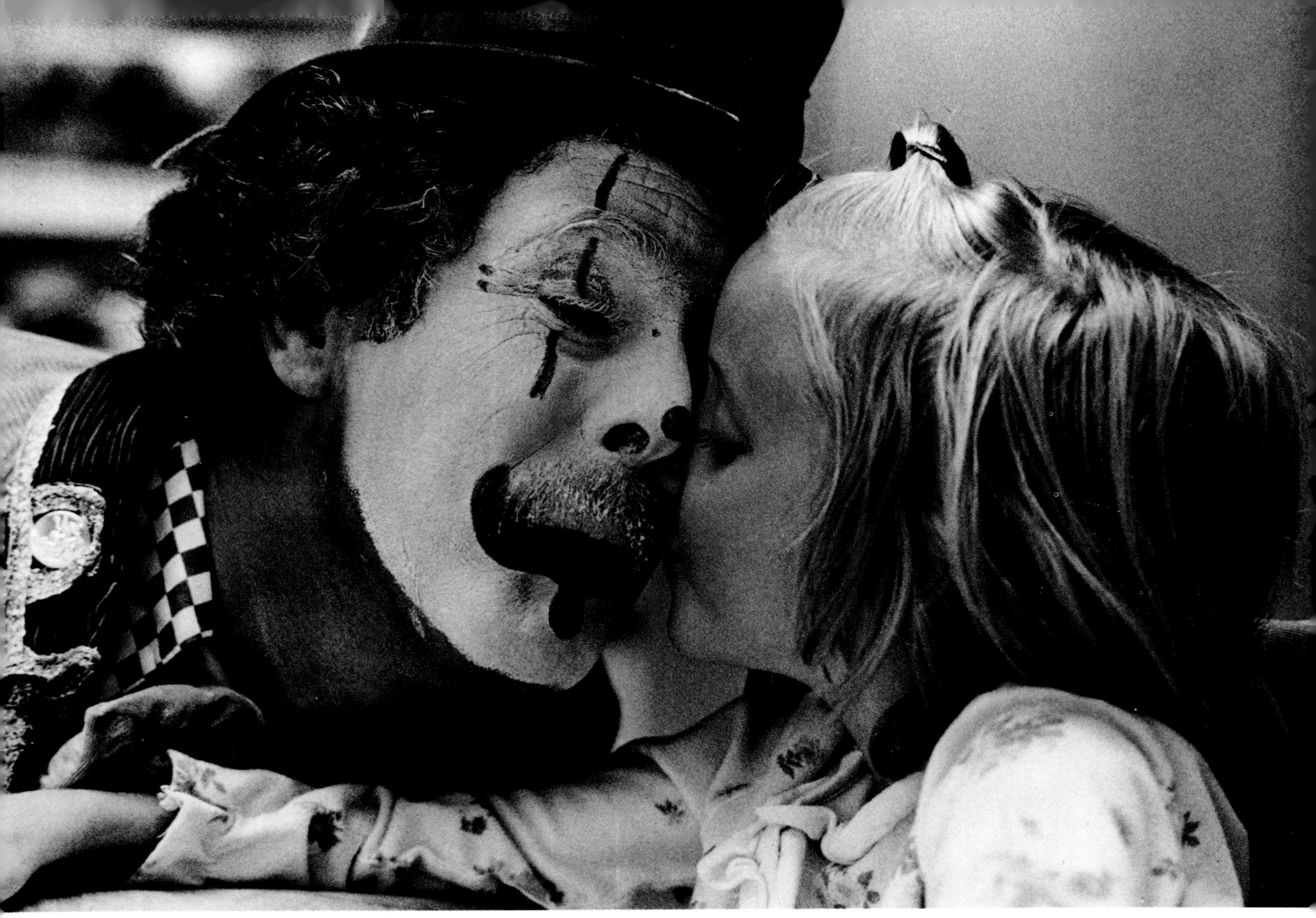

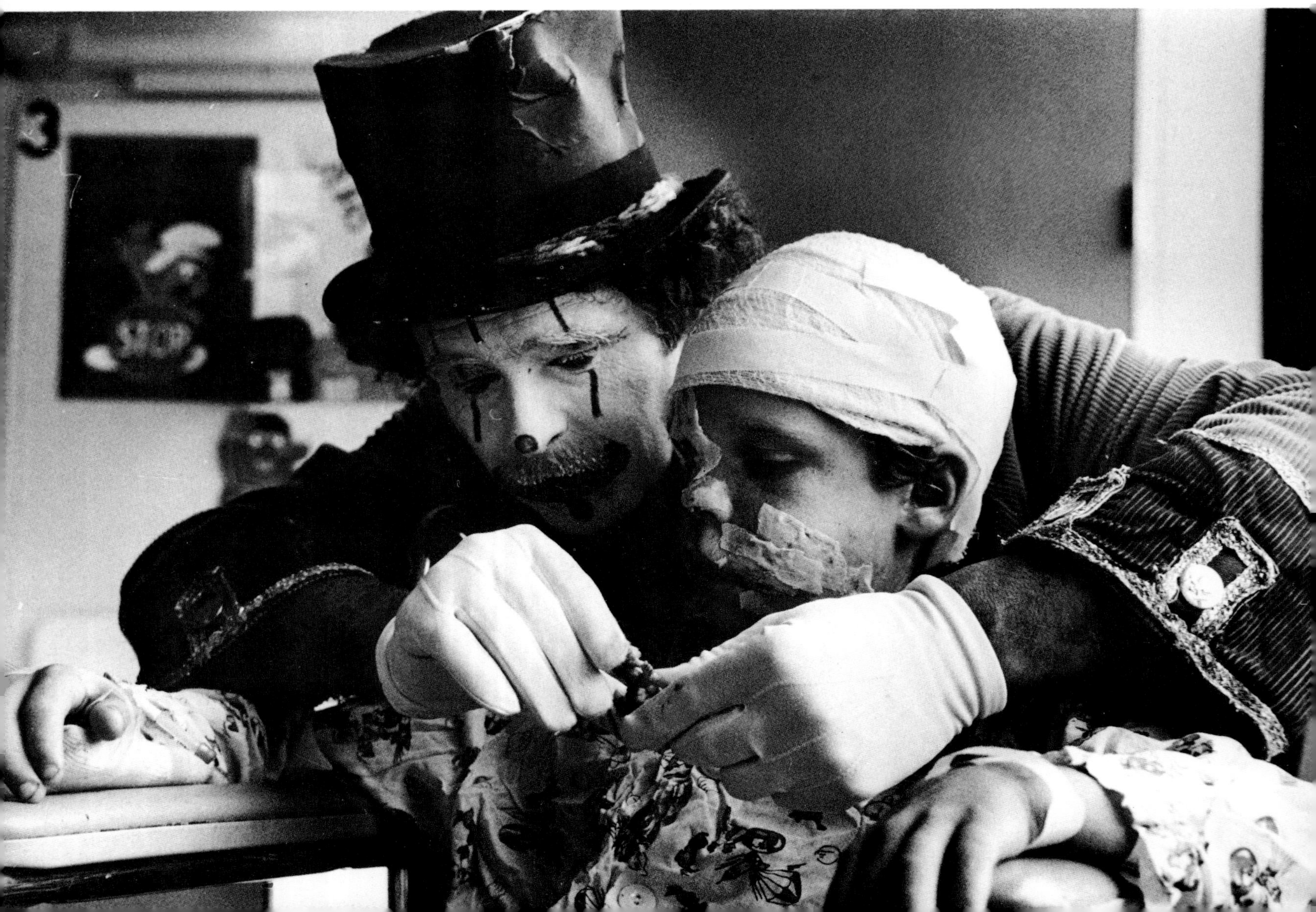
STOP

Clown Minister

"Our intention is deeper than just making people laugh. A clown is an art form that has social feedback. It has therapeutic powers. It grabs the natural child in all of us."

With that theory to guide him, the Rev. William Pindar of Philadelphia swaps the white collar of a minister for the greasepaint of the clown.

And, in traditional baggy pants and whiteface, he comforts the afflicted in cancer wards, psychiatric units, prisons, senior citizen's homes and children's hospitals.

Rusty Kennedy's photos offer a look at the man and his message.

"The clown brings them back and restores their humanity . . . It's life longing for itself."

Footprints on the Moon

By August 1971, man's footprints on the moon were accepted evidence of the spectacular: four expeditions had landed eight men there since the first in July 1969.

The previous space flights, however, had been primarily engineering expeditions. Apollo 15, which blasted off July 29, 1971, was the first moon vehicle whose primary purpose was scientific exploration.

The 12-day trip by mission commander David R. Scott and fellow astronauts James B. Irwin and Alfred M. Worden included three days on the moon with the Lunar Rover—the first man-driven vehicle on the Earth satellite. Among the treasures picked up on the surface by the astronauts were rocks believed to be some 4.6 billion years old!

In this NASA photograph, pilot Irwin salutes while standing beside the U.S. flag planted on the moon. The lunar module is at the center and the rover on the right. Hadley Delta is in the background, looking almost due south. St. George Crater is behind the rover, about three miles away.

By 1983, space travel had developed into a "shuttle" service and astronauts F. Story Musgrave and Donald H. Peterson were able to float about in the cargo bay of the Challenger during an April mission. On their "space walk," they were attached to the shuttle by tethers.

The next year, astronaut Bruce McCandless unhooked a lifeline and became the first human to fly untethered in space, on Feb. 7, 1984. He used a gas-powered jet-pack to propel himself outside the Challenger.

"That may have been one small step for Neil," McCandless said, referring to Neil Armstrong's words upon becoming the first man on the moon in 1969, "but it's a heck of a big leap for me."